The Ultimate Clarinet Book for Beginners

How to Play the Clarinet with Precision, Passion and Pulse

by Maggie Gray

In memory of Bernard Cash

of Bridlington, Yorkshire

1935 – 1988

Always on the beat!

For trade orders, please contact Take Note Music Ltd at:
takenotemusic@outlook.com

ISBN: 978-1-9997837-0-9

First published 2017 by Take Note Music Ltd.

Typeset for Take Note Music Ltd by RAMM Enterprises Limited.

Graphics – by Caroline Scott www.carolinescott.net
Illustrations – by Emily Brinkley www.emilybrinkley.com
Instrument Photography – by Jonathan Hernandez
http://elpoderdelalente.wixsite.com/portfolio
https://es.linkedin.com/in/jonathan-hdez-arbelo

Printed in the UK by Bell and Bain.

CONTENTS

Foreword

The foundations are the most vital part of any building, be it a humble cowshed or a mighty skyscraper; so it is with beginning to play an instrument.

This book devotes the first two chapters to every conceivable aspect of the assembly and manipulation of the clarinet; standing and sitting positions, breathing, and, most usefully, instructions on opening and folding a music stand!

As we progress with the basics of fingering, articulation, music theory and all the rest, it is clear that the author has had many years of experience in teaching at all levels, and professional playing of the highest standard in every style of music.

I am now in my eighties and near the end of my teaching career, but I have one ambition left. I would like my final pupil to be one who has read every word of this book, thoroughly digested it, and is putting every aspect of its advice into practice. Surely that is not too much to ask!

Paul Harvey

Formerly Professor of Clarinet,

Royal Military School of Music, Kneller Hall and Trinity College of Music.

Lifetime Achievement Award, International Clarinet Association.

Preface

ABOUT THIS BOOK

Welcome to *The Ultimate Clarinet Book for Beginners*. Here is your recipe for clarinet success, fun and satisfaction, your 'how to play', your reference guide, your problem solver, your all in one musical package!

Whether you have opened this book feeling excited to discover all about your new instrument or you're disappointed because you're completely stuck with your playing, this book will help you to discover that clarinet playing can be made easy, is a complete joy and that YOU have the potential to be a good player.

Playing and reading music isn't a big, complicated mystery – it's simple when you know what you are doing. At the beginning, for example, there are so many important things to learn, like how to push the air through the instrument evenly and avoid squeaking, and how to make sense of all those symbols in the written music. I can assure you that they are all easy. We just need to make sure that everything is in place; then your sound and your playing will flow, and you will love playing the clarinet!

This book is for both READING AND DOING. Through creative instructions and practical exercises, you are encouraged to bring your music to life by sensing the pulse, feeling the rhythm and breathing with the natural phrasing. You will learn from a position of real understanding as you develop skills to make the best sound and become musically literate. Your playing will feel easy and relaxed as you appreciate that music is to be experienced and sensed, and that it is so much more than a thinking skill.

Trying to combine all the steps at once is impossible, and the initial stages are a delicate time when all kinds of unhelpful habits can creep in – habits that can impair development and create disillusionment in the future. The secret is to absorb the learning, step by step, one thing at a time, and you will feel delighted to discover how everything fits together like a jigsaw to make playing easy.

This is more than a book: it's a system of learning that will give you the confidence to play, read, understand and interpret independently, and draw on your personal musicianship to express yourself.

ABOUT MAGGIE GRAY

I have written this book after a lifetime career in the music industry. For 23 years, I had the privilege of working full time alongside the top musicians in London, in television, radio, orchestras and primarily in London's West End theatres, both as a woodwind player and Musical Director. In later years, I've become an experienced teacher and a real enthusiast for teaching people of all ages to play the clarinet. Being able to combine a professional perspective with considerable teaching experience has enabled me to develop a system of teaching which has had fantastic results for my many students and I believe this can be of help to you too.

I wrote this because I believe that most people can play to a good standard for themselves. When the normal challenges occur, beginners frequently give up and will often hold onto the opinion 'I'm not musical' for the rest of their life. The challenges at the beginning are always technical – they have nothing to do with being musical and they can be sorted out with a little patience.

If you are a brand-new player or you've been playing for a while, and experiencing some difficulties, you need to read this book now! Work on all the bite-size tips and make sure you practise only those helpful habits that will develop strong foundation skills on which you can build your playing in the future.

With best wishes for your musical success and enjoyment,

How to Use This Book

You are about to become a creative artist as well as a smarter clarinet player.

By the time you have finished this book and practised the exercises, you will be using far more of your musical potential than you have ever dreamed you could.

You will learn how to make your playing easier, more relaxed and enjoyable and you will feel amazed at the simplicity of clarinet playing!

There is no reason to struggle with the clarinet in any way. I'm going to make this process easy for you, and make sure your experience is fun and as pleasurable as possible. I want to you to get going and enjoying playing in the shortest possible time.

Here you will learn the fundamental skills of playing. Fundamental skills are those you need today and every single time you play! You will learn how to make a great sound, play with a pulse, develop strong listening skills and you will know how to read music as easily as reading a book. Everything is broken down into tiny understandable pieces so that you find playing easy.

Read this book straight through, and use it as a reference. You will find all the material invaluable both in the initial stages of learning and as you progress through later stages.

Everything here is important, and it is chronological, so I strongly advise that you take this book slowly. Go from the beginning to the end and do not miss any parts out at any stage.

Play full out! Though you may see this book as primarily for reading, it is packed with small vital exercises that add up to you achieving your goals. It doesn't matter how small the task, please do it. Whether you are asked to stand up and march on the spot to sense a pulse, push a strong column of air through your clarinet or count a rhythm out loud – when you are asked to do an exercise do it with as much passion and energy as you possibly can. An excellent sound and the ability to play and read with confidence will be on the way.

Part One, 'A Strong Start', delivers what it says. It's about the technical things to get going. You will learn all you need to know about your instrument – how it works, how to handle it in the best possible way to make the best possible sound and how to care for it and keep yourself safe. Chapter 4 teaches a good range of notes in the chalumeau and throat registers and how to approach the higher notes. You will learn tips and tricks to achieve the different notes technically and will address the hand positions to make sure you play them as efficiently as possible. This chapter is mostly for your reference as you progress through following stages.

Part Two, 'Read, Count, Play, Enjoy', is about bringing out the musician in you, so your listeners will want to tap their foot to your playing – just as when you enjoy your favorite tunes. It's all very well having the technical skills to play but they are only your playing tools through which you express your music.

You may notice certain underlying themes appearing in the teaching. The most vital one is that of 'pulse'. Through these chapters, you will learn how to set the pulse, 'sense' it within you, and breathe with the natural phrasing of the music, just like when you sing a song. You will bring your playing to life from the onset.

The first chapters in this section gradually introduce you to the musical signs and symbols and teach you how to count the rhythms and become musically literate to the level of reading quavers and dotted notes.

In Chapter 10, 'PLAY the Next Tunes' you will learn the **'Three Step System for Reading Music'** which you can apply to the reading of any tune in the future.

Chapter 11 **'Whoops! Got a Problem?'** is invaluable for both now and for a long time in the future as it provides the answers and solutions to most of the common challenges.

'Practice is Magic', Chapter 12, explains exactly why practising is important, and you'll get lots of different ideas to keep you motivated and enjoying your playing. The **'Daily Practice Plan for All Round Development'** is about what and how to practise. It is structured, so you get the most benefit and progress from your time.

Take special notice of the **'Practising Checklist for Beginners'**: it is about the technical skills learned in Part One. Beginners frequently forget many of their best playing habits when they have their mind on reading the tune and of course, this can lead to unnecessary problems.

The checklist is intentionally displayed over two pages and I suggest that you open the book at this page and keep it close to your music stand for the first months of learning.

Refer to this frequently to make sure you practise only those helpful habits that will continuously strengthen your playing and improve your sound.

Though detailed in the last module **'On a Final Note'**, one of the best assets of this book is the **FREE video course 'Clarinet Kickstart'**. Make sure you access this online as it will supplement your learning considerably.

'Clarinet Kickstart' lasts about 1 hour 20 minutes in total. It is the beginner's introduction to a much longer series of lessons. Being audio-visual it will get you off to a strong start very quickly, both with sound production and literacy skills. Although presented for a younger audience I am assured that Anthony the Ant is extremely popular with adults also.

Let's get going!

CHAPTER 1

Know Your Instrument

- Have Fun with the Clarinet
- Body Parts of the Clarinet and Mouthpiece
- Ten Top Reed Facts
- Three Essential Ligature Points
- Middle Joint Alert!
- Perfect Assembly for Perfect Playing
- Why Clean a Clarinet?
- Safety and Care All Round

Have Fun with the Clarinet

The clarinet is versatile because it can play in all sorts of groups, orchestras and bands, and even perform as a solo instrument. It can also be used to play many styles of music such as jazz, classical and pop – how cool! You may have in mind some of the kinds of groups you would like to play in – maybe a classical orchestra or a jazz group, or you might like to get together with friends and play chamber music at home. Whatever your goal, there are many possibilities, and your exciting adventure is just ahead of you!

The clarinet has evolved to an exceptionally high standard over many years. It has a fantastic system of holes, springs, pads, keys, and corks – and it's designed for us to play with ease.

We are lucky, as the modern-day clarinet is well in tune, fits perfectly into the natural position of our hands and fingers, and feels comfortable to handle. Made of either wood or some form of resin or plastic, the instrument is narrow at the mouthpiece end and very gradually widens towards the bell at the bottom.

By becoming familiar with the numerous parts and understanding how the clarinet works, you will appreciate how perfect assembly and natural handling of the instrument leads to easy sound production and fluent technique.

This chapter explains:

- Why it's essential to treat the individual parts with care.
- How to make reeds last.
- How to put the instrument together quickly and easily.
- How to clean and care for the clarinet.
- How to keep both yourself and your instrument safe.

Do not get caught up in any technical detail, as your understanding will strengthen as you progress through the book. Fabulous clarinet playing evolves over time, so above all, it is most important to have fun with the clarinet!

Body Parts of the Clarinet and Mouthpiece

The Assembled Clarinet

The Mouthpiece →

The Barrel →

The Upper Middle Joint →

The Lower Middle Joint →

The Bell →

The Mouthpiece Parts

The mouthpiece has three parts, each with its own important function.

The Reed sets up the vibrating air which travels through the clarinet to produce the sound.

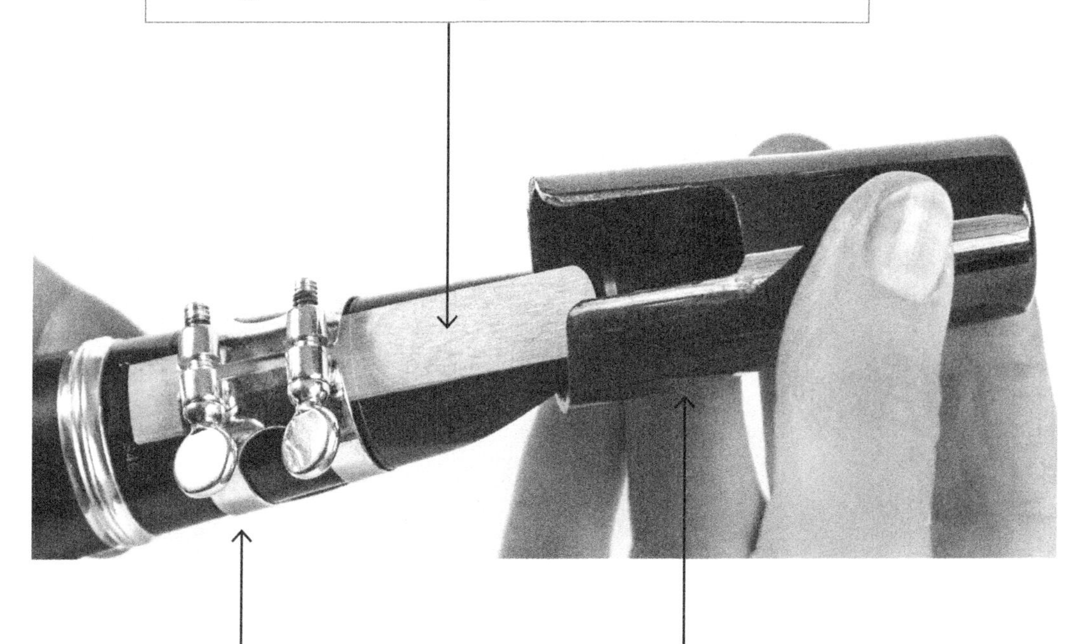

The Ligature keeps the reed securely in position on the mouthpiece whilst at the same time allowing it to vibrate to its full potential.

The Cap protects the reed and the fine mouthpiece tip whenever the clarinet is not in use.

Mouthpieces are made of ebonite (hard rubber), glass, and plastic. Individual players choose a mouthpiece according to the type of sound they wish to make, but ebonite mouthpieces are popular as they are highly resonant.

Remember the names of the different sections of the mouthpiece. Notice the rails and the tip are thin and delicate – these need careful handling as they play an important part in producing a high-quality sound.

The **mouthpiece tip** is protected by the mouthpiece cap when not in use.

The **rails** of the mouthpiece are equal on both sides.

The **reed table** is perfectly flat. It's the place where the reed sits.

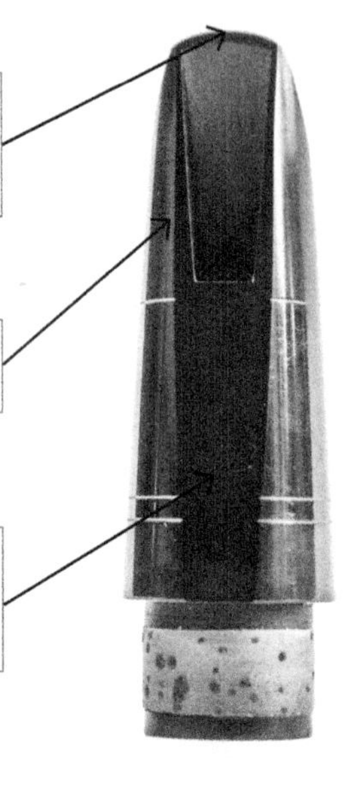

The **beak** is the top part of the mouthpiece where the top teeth sit.

The **tip opening** is a measurement. It's the distance between the reed and the tip of the mouthpiece.

The **lay curve** goes from the point at which the mouthpiece bends away from the reed table to the tip.

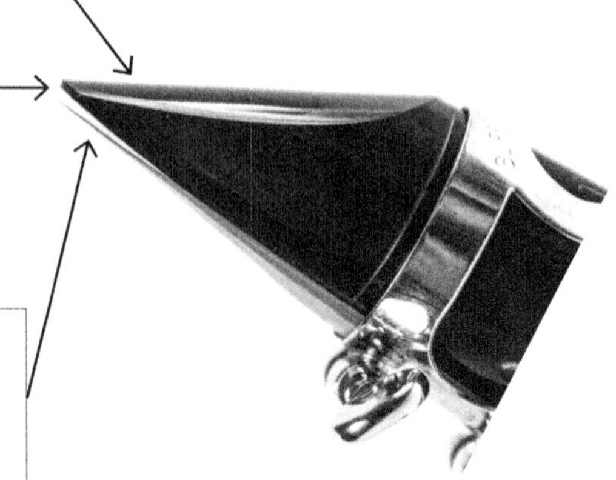

Ten Top Reed Facts

The reed is a vital part of the clarinet. It doesn't matter how expensive or beautiful or shiny the clarinet is, if the reed is not in good condition and working well, the clarinet will not sound good. Remember these top ten reed facts:

1. Most reeds are made from pieces of cane

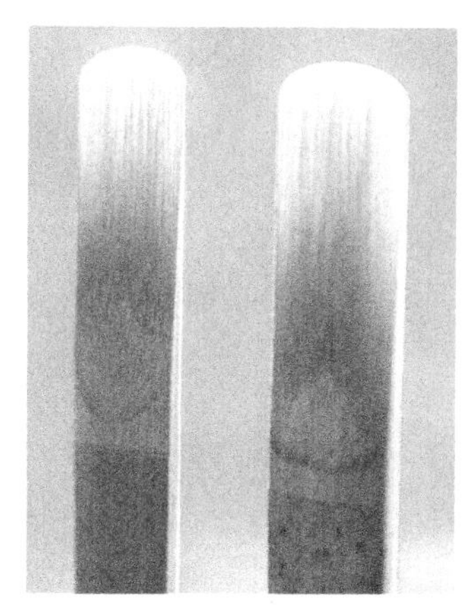

The reed is a part of a large piece of reed grass like bamboo cane, and grows in countries with warm climates such as southern France, which has a reputation for producing the finest quality. The reed is cut to fit the clarinet mouthpiece and is shaved gradually thinner and thinner towards the tip. It's possible to buy synthetic reeds, or reeds coated in plastic, though this is not usually recommended for a beginner.

2. Reeds can last a long time but they do break

With extra care and careful handling, reeds can last for a while, but there's no point feeling upset or frustrated if a reed splits, chips, or stops working!

3. Reeds are handled by their base

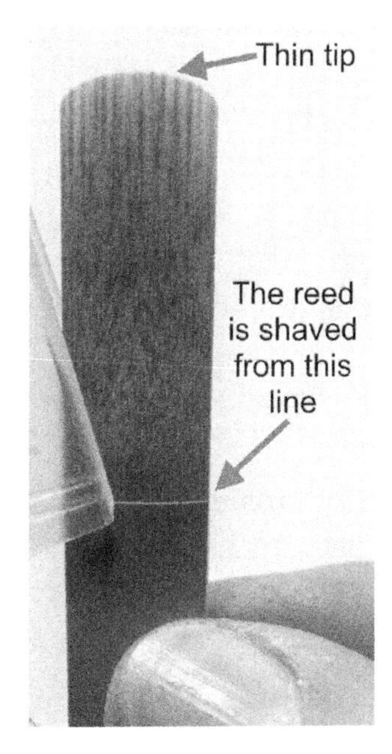

By holding a reed up to the light, you'll be able to see how the reed is shaved, and how delicate and thin the tip is. By handling the reed by the base (the blade), where it is the thickest, it is possible to avoid touching the tip which can be easily damaged.

4. Reeds are graded

Reeds are graded by their thickness and strength – soft, medium and hard. The lower numbers indicate the thinnest reeds, which are the softest and easiest to play. The recommended reed strength for a beginner is usually number 1½ – soft reeds enable a beginner to play with a small amount of effort.

5. Moist reeds work best

A moist reed works better than a dry one. Most players choose to put the tip of the reed in their mouth for a few seconds, but it can also be placed into a small glass of water to make it damp before playing. Whichever method is used, the reed must be just moist, never soggy, when it is placed onto the mouthpiece.

6. The flat side of the reed meets the flat reed table of the mouthpiece

The thin end of the reed lines up with the thin end of the mouthpiece. The flat side of the reed rests on the flat reed table – easy!

7. Reeds vibrate

The reed and mouthpiece together make a valve that rapidly opens and closes as air is pushed through the clarinet mouthpiece. The air sets into vibration and travels through the clarinet to produce the fabulous sound.

8. Reeds need drying after use

The reed and clarinet body need drying at the end of each playing session, for both hygiene reasons and good care. After drying, the reed is carefully put back into the reed case or reassembled back onto the mouthpiece. It will then dry out ready for the next playing session with minimum warping.

9. Reeds are ALWAYS protected by the mouthpiece cap when not in use

Replace the mouthpiece cap immediately after the practice has stopped to prevent the tip of the reed catching on something. Make this a habit from the onset. The cap protects the mouthpiece tip as well as the reed – these are both extremely delicate and need special consideration.

10. Reed tips sometimes warp

A warped reed can usually be straightened by soaking it in water for a while, then placing the flat side down on a piece of glass and allowing it to dry.

With special reed care and consideration:

- You will put your reed on without chipping it.
- You will be able to adjust your reed quickly and save lots of time so you can get on with playing.
- Your reed will last longer.
- You will save money (it's expensive to replace broken reeds all the time).
- You will produce a high-quality sound efficiently.

Learn how to set the reed on the mouthpiece in the module 'Perfect Assembly for Perfect Playing'.

Three Essential Ligature Points

The ligature holds the reed on to the mouthpiece. Over the years, manufacturers have designed many styles, striving to achieve minimum contact between the reed and ligature, thus allowing the reed to vibrate to its maximum potential.

Ligatures come in different shapes, sizes and materials. Some are designed to be adjusted by the screws at the back of the mouthpiece, on the opposite side to the reed, while the conventional styles have the screws on the same side. By observing the space where the reed fits within the ligature it will be obvious which way round to set the adjusting screws.

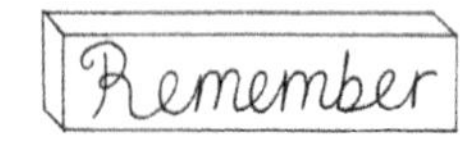

1. The ligature gently holds the reed in place.

The lines on the front and back of the reed are fibers which extend from the base to the tip. These fibers that vibrate at the tip of the reed are those same fibers held at the base by the ligature. A reed that is held too tightly at the base by the ligature will not function to its potential, so it very important not to nip the base of the reed.

2. The ligature sits on the thick unshaven part of the reed.

Notice the line going horizontally across the reed, where the shaving starts. The best place for the ligature to sit is just below this line, on the thick base of the reed. Putting it too high above this line prevents the reed working well.

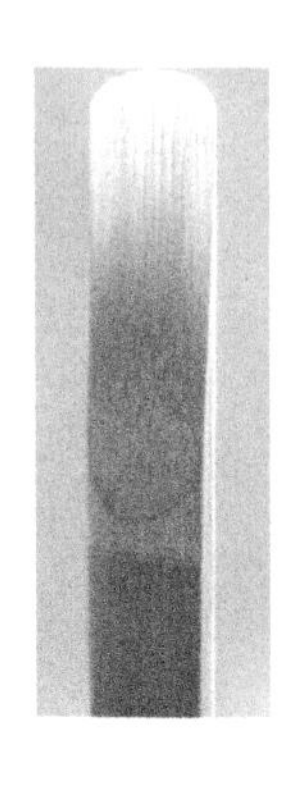

The three ligature positions below will **not** allow the reed to vibrate to its maximum potential and make the best sound.

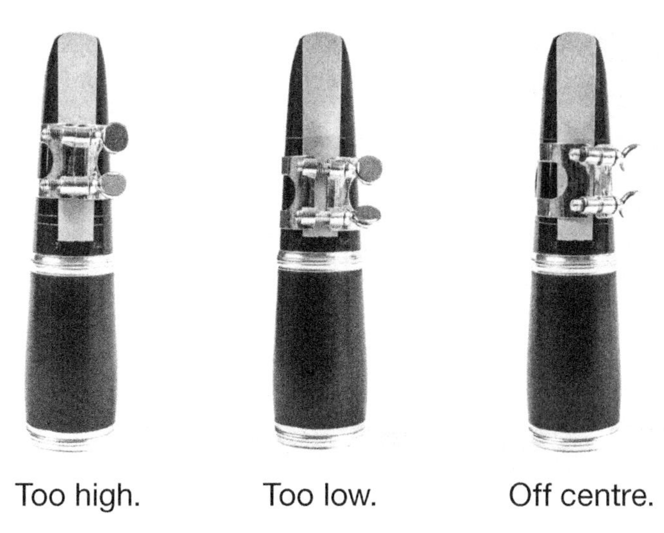

Too high. Too low. Off centre.

3. The ligature sits central to the reed.

The ligature usually has screws that adjust at the side of the reed. Place the join of the ligature in the middle of the reed then adjust the screws. If your ligature adjusts at the back of the mouthpiece, on the opposite side to the reed, make sure the join of the ligature is in the centre of the back before tightening it.

These ligatures are perfectly placed. They are at the perfect height and the screws support the reed in a balanced way.

Middle Joint Alert!

The **right-hand** fingers operate the **lower middle joint:**

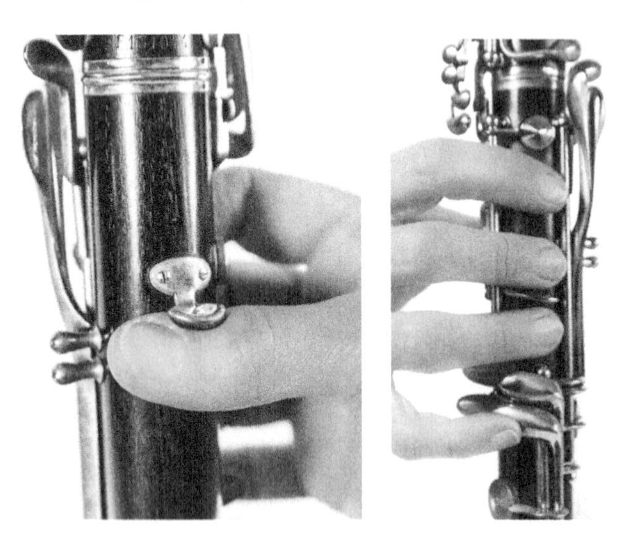

From the back of the lower middle joint, **the right thumb supports the whole body of the clarinet**. You can't mistake the thumb rest - it's the only bit that sticks out. The player keeps the thumb straight and places it underneath the rest **between the nail and the knuckle**. The first three fingers cover the three holes and press the ring keys that go around these holes. The fourth finger operates the four keys at the bottom.

The **left-hand** fingers operate the **upper middle joint:**

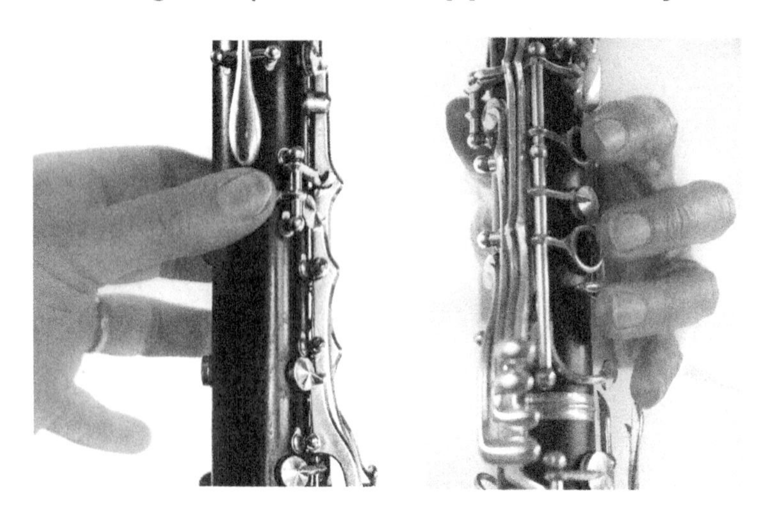

The left thumb covers the hole at the back of the joint and works the large speaker key (also called the register key).

At the front of the joint, the three large holes and the two ring keys that go around them are covered by the player's first three fingers. The fourth finger operates the side keys, one next to the third finger and the three long side keys on the lower joint.

Alert! Notice the linkage keys on both the middle joints.

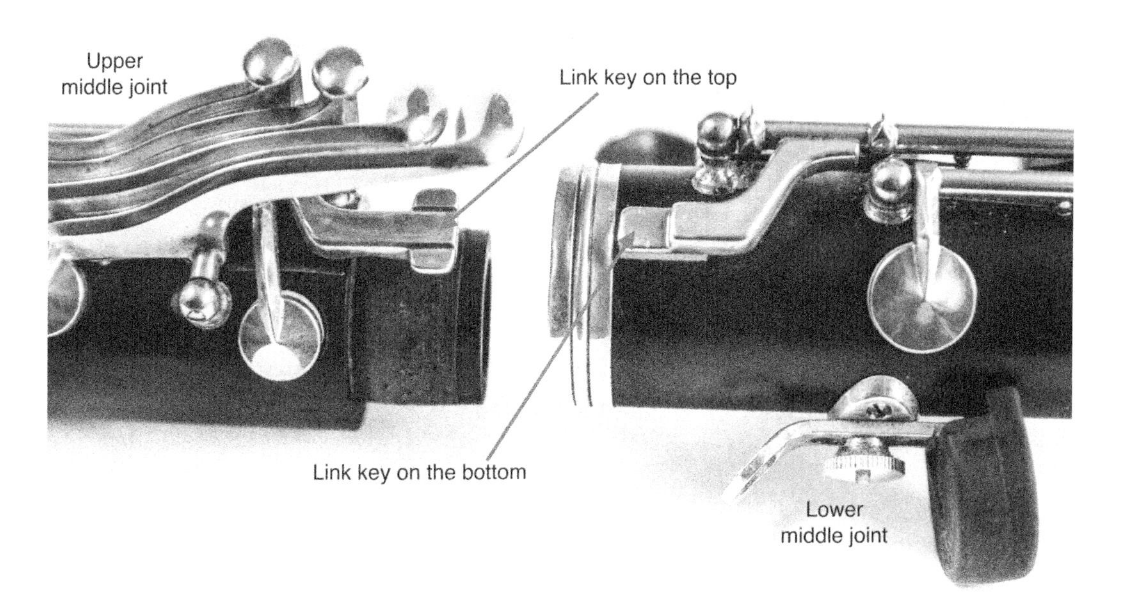

These keys are known as either 'Bridge Keys' or 'Link Keys'. Together, they form the link (or the bridge) between the two joints. It is worth giving these two keys special attention at the beginning, as they can so easily become bent if not handled well. The link key on the bottom joint goes underneath the link key on the top joint. When they are exactly in place, the holes on both the joints are in the perfect playing position and the mechanism is synchronised.

Alert! Notice the side keys near the first fingers.

The side keys usually give beginners, especially the young ones whose hands have not fully-grown, some challenges at the beginning of learning. It is important to avoid accidentally touching these keys with the sides of the first fingers when putting the hands around the clarinet – they can be responsible for many squeaks. By keeping both hands in the shape of a letter 'C' around the clarinet, the player can avoid touching these keys unnecessarily.

Perfect Assembly for Perfect Playing

Take your time to learn to put the clarinet together and protect the delicate keys. By assembling your instrument and reed perfectly you will make your playing easier.

Grease the corks

The corks at the end of some of the joints ensure a tight seal when the clarinet parts are together. New corks are fat, making the joints stiff and difficult to put together at first. Greasing helps them to slide together easily.

You may have been provided with some cork grease when you purchased your instrument, either in a small pot or in stick form. If you haven't got any, use a small amount of household petroleum jelly to grease the corks.

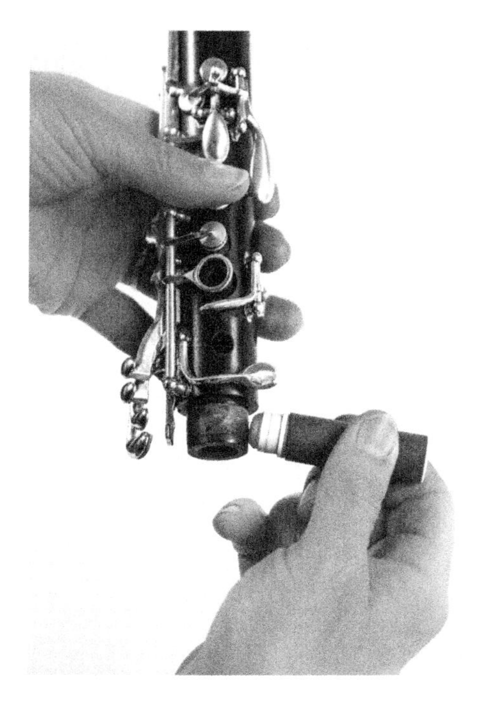

Smooth a small amount around the cork with the tip of your finger, and you will find that the joints slide together easily. Try not to get grease on the body of the clarinet as this will make it sticky. Only apply cork grease when the joints are stiff. After a period of playing the corks will settle, and you will need to grease less frequently.

Watch the module
'Assembly and Clarinet Care'
in your free online course
'Clarinet Kickstart'

Assemble the middle joints

Pick up the **upper middle joint** – the smallest of the two middle joints. Point the long speaker key at the back, upwards.

Place this joint in **the left hand** with the holes upwards so you can see them.

Curl the first three fingers around the body and press the ring keys that go around the holes. As you press the ring keys, the link key lifts to enable the lower link key to go underneath it.

Place the **lower middle joint** in the **right hand** with the thumb rest upwards (the bit that sticks out).

Put the joints closely together so the holes are in a line. Pinpoint the link/bridge keys on both middle joints that will join. Keeping the left hand still, slowly move the bottom joint towards the top. **Making small movements twist the bottom joint a little right, left**, right, left till the link keys are perfectly aligned.

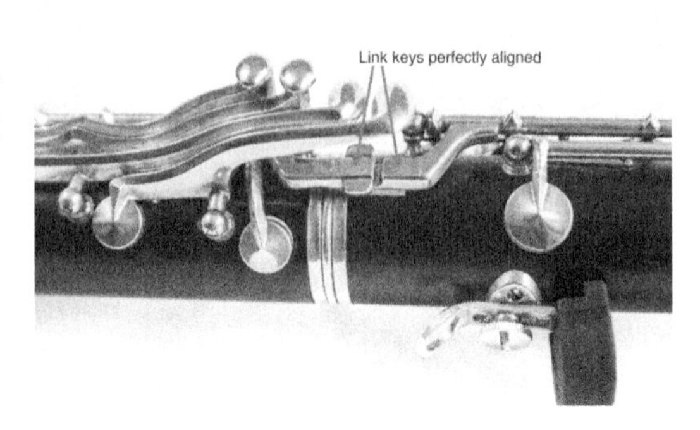

Lift the left-hand fingers off the ring keys, allowing the link key on the top joint to drop over the link key on the bottom joint. The mechanism of the clarinet is now synchronised.

Do not allow the long side keys to touch by fully twisting the joints round, as this may bend both the link keys and the long side keys.

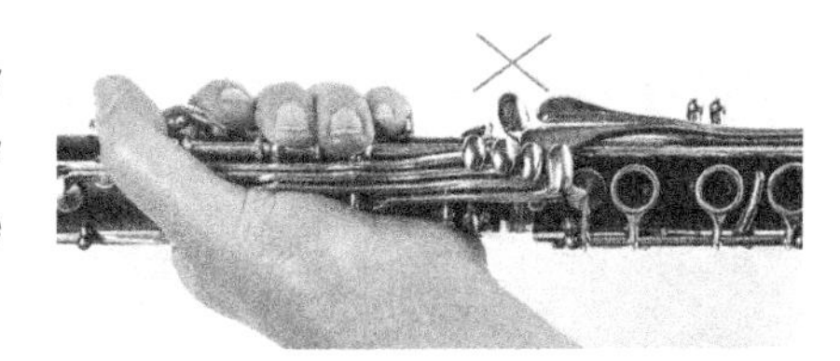

Add the bell

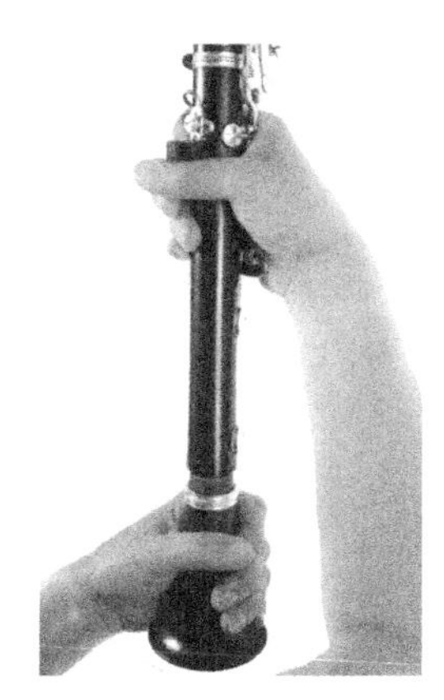

This bit is easy! There's just one point that I would like you to learn, and it's an important part of good clarinet care. When putting the bell on the clarinet, hold the instrument by the bottom joint to screw on the bell. Do not hold the top joint of the clarinet when adding the bell, because it may cause movement between the middle joints, again resulting in bent keys.

Add the barrel

The barrel is the small piece similar in shape to a beer barrel. It fits onto the top joint. Similar advice applies to putting on the bell. Hold the body of the instrument by the top joint when adding the barrel to prevent movement in the middle.

Add the mouthpiece and reed

The reed must be perfectly placed on the mouthpiece and secured by the ligature to enable it to make the best sound. There are various ways to put a reed on a clarinet, so learn and practice all these methods and then choose the most efficient way for you!

Firstly, there are **THREE positions in which you could hold the clarinet when putting the reed on.**

1. **Screw the mouthpiece into the barrel and put the reed on from there.** The advantage of putting the reed on with only a small part of the clarinet in your hand, is that you don't have the extra weight of the instrument to deal with. Once the reed is assembled, you can then put the barrel onto the main body of the instrument. Align the reed with the large speaker key at the back of the clarinet.

OR

2. **Lay the assembled clarinet on your lap to put on the reed.** Line the flat reed table with the long speaker key at the back of the upper middle joint before you put your reed on to the mouthpiece. Usually, young clarinet players prefer this way as the weight of the instrument is on the lap, leaving both hands free to deal with the reed and the ligature.

OR

3. **Put the fully-assembled body of the clarinet upright, with the bell either on your knee or your chair.** Your hands will then be free to deal with the reed. Align the reed table of the mouthpiece with the long speaker key, before placing the reed.

THEN EITHER:

Put the reed on first, then the ligature:

- Hold the mouthpiece with your left hand.
- With the right, handle the reed by the thick base and the sides as you

maneuver it into place on the reed table – flat side down. **Make sure the sides of the reed are parallel with the rails of the mouthpiece and the top of the reed is perfectly in line with the tip of the mouthpiece.**

- Press the base of the reed firmly with the left-hand thumb to keep it in place.

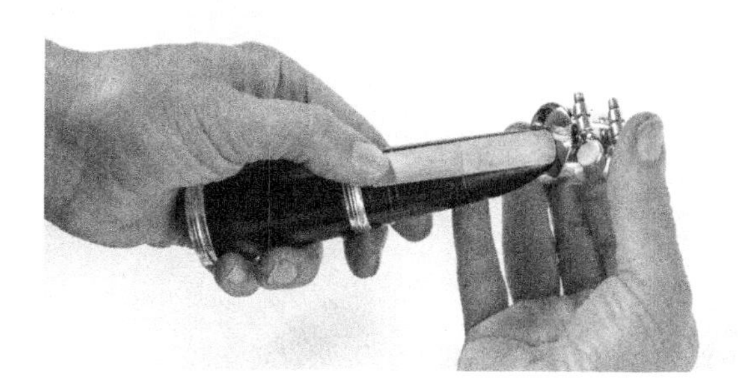

- Link **the bottom of the ligature with the back of the mouthpiece and slowly slide it down and over the top**, completely avoiding the reed tip.

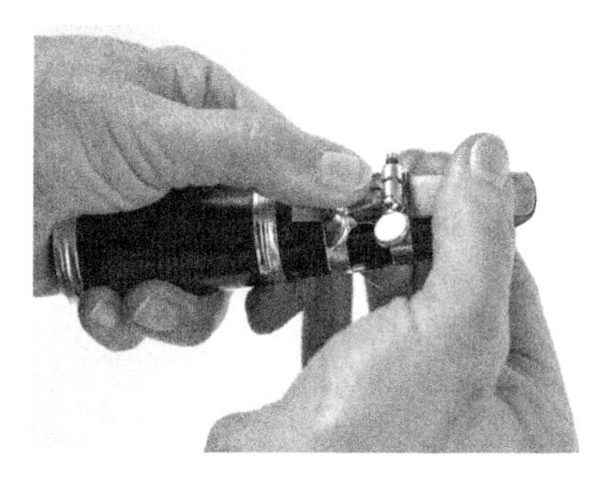

- **Test the height of the reed by pressing it firmly with the flat thumb placed underneath the tip. When you can see the faint black line of the mouthpiece just above the tip, you have set your reed correctly.**

- Make sure the ligature is central, and sitting below the shaved part of the reed then adjust the screws to keep the reed in place.

OR

Put the ligature on first – then the reed:

- Slide the ligature over the mouthpiece.
- Hold in the left hand and push the ligature up a little.
- Slip the reed behind the ligature onto the flat reed table, so it is perfectly straight with the sides of the mouthpiece.

- Check the height of the reed. **Make any adjustments by handling it by the base or the sides. Avoid any temptation to touch the fine reed tip with your fingers.**
- Adjust the ligature height and the tension of the screws so the reed stays in place and at the same time is not nipped and restricted.

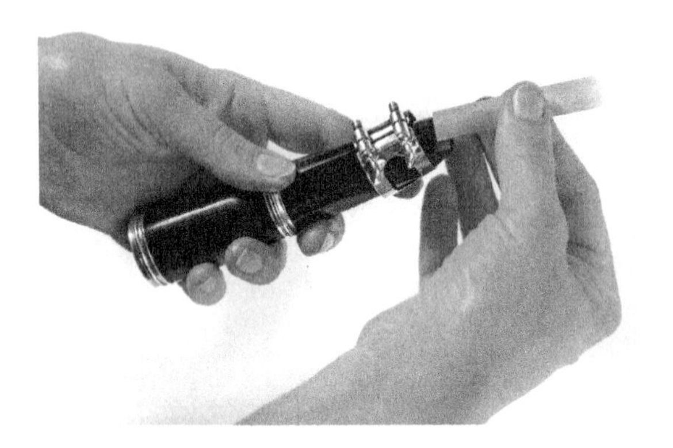

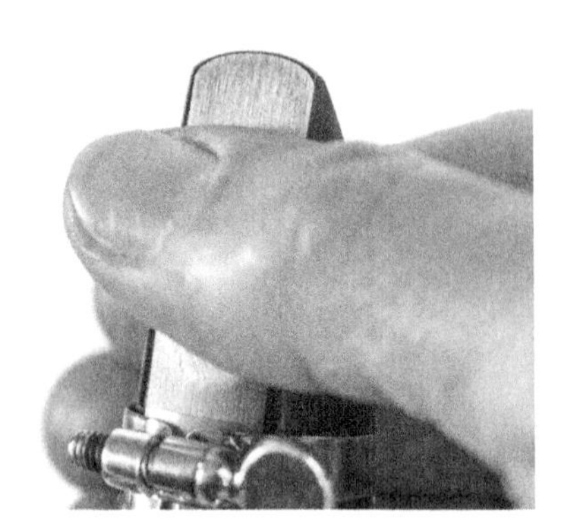

Add the mouthpiece cap

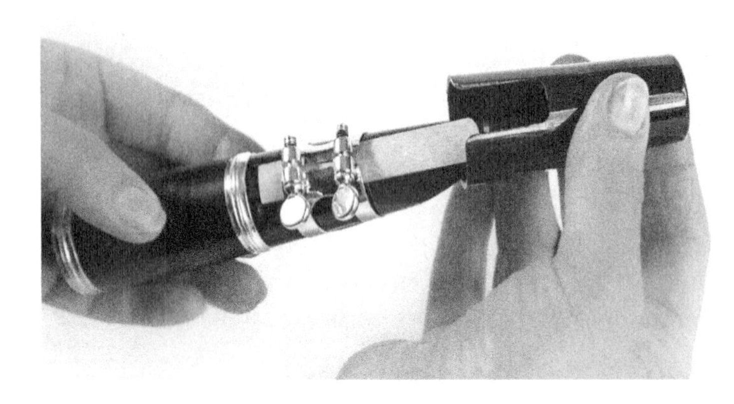

It is important to protect the reed and mouthpiece tip when the clarinet is not being played. To put the cap on, touch the back of the mouthpiece beak with the bottom of the cap. Slowly slide the cap down the back of the mouthpiece, to **avoid the reed and mouthpiece tip completely.**

Be patient and take your time!

It may take time to feel comfortable putting a reed on a clarinet. Frequently, beginners rush when putting their instrument together and forget to put the reed on in the best way. They then struggle, get into bad habits forcing the sound out, and find it difficult to make a good sound.

Make playing easy and comfortable by practising putting your reed on in the best possible way, every time you play.

Quick reed recap:

- Handle the reed by the base or the sides only.
- Moisten the reed before placing it on to the mouthpiece.
- Place the ligature underneath the line from which the reed is shaved.
- Adjust the screws of the ligature firmly without nipping the reed.
- Place the ligature central to the reed and mouthpiece.

Enjoy your Playing!

Why Clean a Clarinet?

Beginner clarinetists may neglect to dry out their instrument after a practice session, resulting in an unpleasant build-up of moisture deposits inside the mouthpiece.

Not cleaning the clarinet is simply not cool, it's plain unhygienic!

The temperature of the air when it travels through the clarinet is warmer than the temperature of the instrument. This air condenses inside the bore and makes not only the mouthpiece wet but also the whole of the inside of the body too. Make drying this condensation a good habit from the onset – something you do automatically and quickly at the end of every single playing session.

My favorite way is simple – it involves minimum equipment, and uses neither abrasive or chemical cleaners.

All you need for cleaning your clarinet is a 'pull-through' (also known as a 'swab') **and a soft cloth or duster.** An alternative is to use a brush.

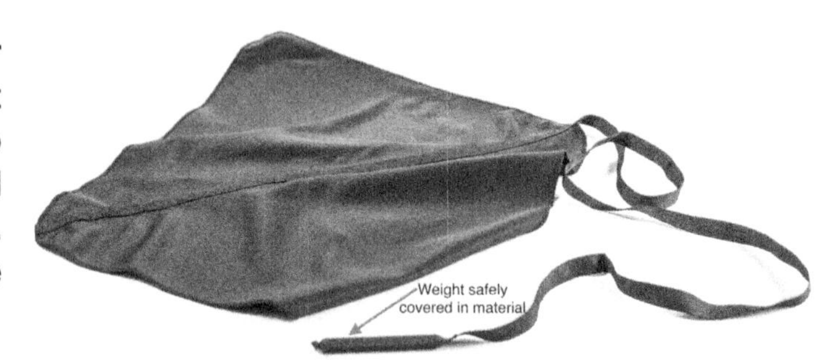

New clarinets usually have a pull-through provided. Your pull-through will be a piece of absorbent material with a long string, which has a weight at the end. The weight will usually be a small piece of metal or hard plastic covered by the material of the string. A rough, uncovered weight may scratch the bore – **make sure your weight is covered by the material of the pull-through.**

Everyday quick dry and clean.

- Hold the top joint and **twist off the barrel and mouthpiece.**
- Drop the weight at the end of the pull-through, down the top joint through to the bell. **Pull the weight underneath the bell and bring the cloth**

through the body of the clarinet. Take care to feed the material in untangled, so it does not get stuck in the bore on the way down. Do this a few times if your clarinet is particularly wet. Some players choose to drop the pull-through in from the bell. I prefer the other way because if the clarinet is excessively wet it may avoid bringing water back into the tone holes.

- Dismantle the body of the clarinet. **Dry the end recesses of the clarinet joints** by twisting some of the cloth inside the ends.

- Take the reed off the mouthpiece. **Clean inside the mouthpiece** with your finger under the pull-through. Push in the material and turn the cloth gently until dry. Take special care never to scratch the bore inside, or damage the rails and the mouthpiece tip.

- To **dry the reed**, wrap the pull-through cloth over your finger and take the moisture off from the base to the tip end. Completely dry both the front and the back. **Only clean the reed in the direction of the base to the tip.**

- Either **place the reed into a protective case, or back onto your mouthpiece** ready to be used the next time you play.

- Take the soft cloth or duster and gently **take any fingerprints or grease marks off the metal key work and body of the instrument.**

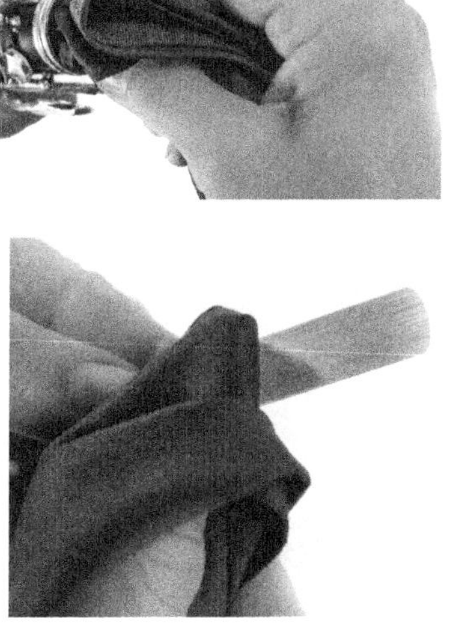

- **Put the clarinet joints into the case**, making sure they are perfectly dry.

Extra cleaning tips:

- **Pull the cloth slowly** through the clarinet to absorb as much moisture as possible.
- **Pull the cloth gently**. The metal from the speaker hole in the top joint sticks out into the bore of the clarinet, and jerky movements may disturb this.
- **Give the mouthpiece special attention**. Sometimes people choose to pull the pull-through cloth right through the mouthpiece to dry it. In this case, do it with great care so you don't damage the rails of the mouthpiece or the delicate tip (the beak). You may choose to dry the mouthpiece by gently pushing the cloth in both ends in turn, and twisting it round.

Now and then:

- Take a tissue to the corks and **clean away any old cork grease and re-apply fresh**. Never have congealed grease on your instrument.
- **Wash the mouthpiece once a week**. Using **lukewarm** water (hot can discolor it), place the mouthpiece under the tap, then dry completely.

Safety and Care All Round

A cherished and cared-for clarinet will be easy to play and makes for a happy musician. Act on the following points to keep yourself and your clarinet safe.

Caring for you:

- When holding the clarinet, **keep the mouthpiece away from your eyes to prevent accidents**. While sitting and not playing, hold the clarinet vertically with your hand around the lower joint, the bell on the knee and the mouthpiece pointing upwards, completely away from the eyes. Alternately, hold the clarinet horizontally, lying across the knee.
- If you are a young player, you may have chosen to use a neck strap. Often, the neckpieces are slightly elasticated for comfort. **Don't be tempted to bounce the clarinet on the sling or wiggle it around from the pivot of the hook on the thumb rest.** The mouthpiece could end up in your eye or someone else's eye.
- **When walking** with the assembled instrument, **hold it down at arm's length.**

Every day clarinet care:

- **Dry the clarinet after each practice session.**
- **Avoid the reed touching the shoulder.** Beginners often look down at the instrument to find the fingerings; then the reed catches the jumper or jacket, and the reed chips.
- **Always protect the reed and the mouthpiece tip with the cap** when not playing.
- **Keep the instrument away from extreme temperatures.** Clarinets left near radiators or in the cold boot of a car overnight may go out of tune, and if the instrument is made of wood, it may crack or split.
- **Do not allow anyone else try your instrument.** They may not handle it well, nor care for it as you do.

Occasional clarinet care:

- **Clean the pads of the clarinet.** Use a piece of paper to blot any moisture and remove any debris. Press the pad down gently on the paper, then pull the paper out taking the debris from underneath the pad. Do this also if the pad is sticky.
- Now and then, **check the tiny screws that are at the ends of pillars and rods**. Over time, the screws sometimes loosen, and it can be easy to lose one if it drops on the floor. Adjust the screws that are loose with a tiny screwdriver.

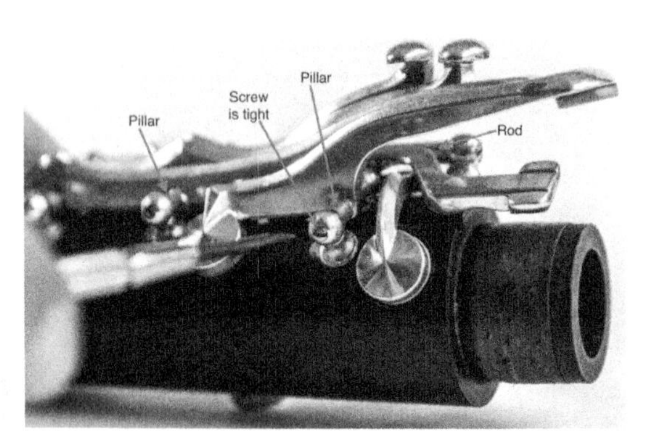

- Occasionally, you may like to **apply a small amount of oil to the screws.** Always use the oil supplied from a music shop for the purpose, as it will dispense from a nozzle and avoid getting oil all over the instrument. Only use the kind of oil that is sold specifically for this purpose.
- **Check out the springs**. A spring may pop off its ledge without warning. Gently ease it back into position, and it will work normally.

- Wooden clarinets are prone to cracking. Obtain advice from the manufacturer regarding the frequency and specific care of a new wooden instrument. In general, **oil the bore of a clarinet twice a week when the instrument is new.** Put some bore oil on an old pull-through and pull this through the clarinet when the instrument is dry. You will see a thin coating of oil, which will prevent moisture going into the wood of the clarinet. The oil is invaluable for preventing cracking. It is not necessary to oil the outside of the clarinet. Do not to get oil on the pads and use special bore oil sold for this purpose.

As with all mechanical things, **a service will be required after a period.** Just as the family car is serviced once a year, the clarinet will need one too. Repairing or adjusting a clarinet is no big deal. There are many instrument repairers throughout the country who perform this specialised job. Rather than tackling a mechanical problem yourself, I would recommend you take the clarinet for an overhaul once every one to two years, or when you feel the instrument is unresponsive. Repairers will not provide a replacement clarinet while yours is serviced, so it is wise to book the job in advance, so the instrument is not sitting in a queue for a long time, leaving you unable to practise.

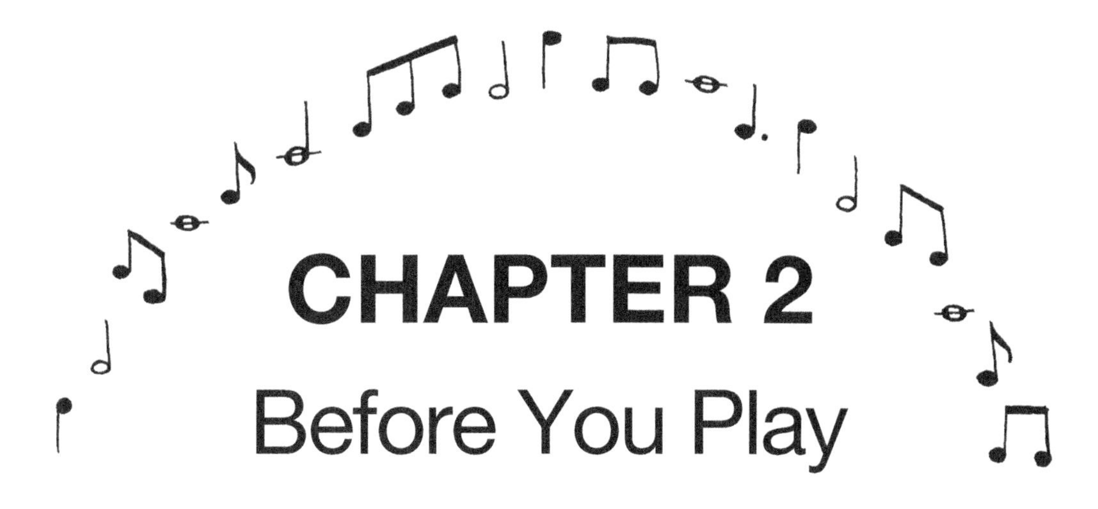

CHAPTER 2

Before You Play

- What's This All About?
- Relaxed and Chilled
- About Air Control
- Four Vital Breathing Exercises
- Sensible Sling Use
- Let's Get Hands-On
- Clarinet Angle
- How to Use a Music Stand
- Rooted Like a Tree
- All Together Now

What's This All About?

Up until now, we have focused on our instrument:

- We know how to keep the clarinet in the best possible condition and how to assemble it in perfect alignment.
- We can set the reed on the mouthpiece and hold it in position with a perfectly placed ligature.
- We now have an instrument that will give us the best chance of producing beautiful music.

Now, let's put the focus on ourselves – on our bodies.

We are even more significant because the music comes 'through' us as we operate this fantastic machine. By being physically relaxed within, we can make sure the experience is as smooth, pleasurable and comfortable as possible.

Great News!
PLAYING THE CLARINET CAN BE MADE EASY!

At the beginning, there are many important things to learn, and they are all simple. When they are all in place at the same time – your playing will flow and YOU WILL LOVE PLAYING THE CLARINET.

Learning all the small skills at once is impossible but by taking things slowly, and learning each small step in turn, you will find that playing is easy and you will be surprised at your musical abilities and how everything fits together perfectly.

This chapter focuses on the important points that we need to know BEFORE we begin to play. By taking the time to address them one by one, it will become apparent how simple they all are and how they fit together like a jigsaw to make the start of playing easy.

Relaxed and Chilled

The calmer and more focused we feel, the better the music sounds – how cool is that?

The whole body is involved with playing the clarinet – how we breathe, sit, stand, and position our arms, hands and fingers are all important. The great news is that by keeping and using the body in the most natural positions, just as it is – the easier it is to play and the better it feels – so the resulting playing is improved, and the player feels inspired, motivated and happy.

Straight back and relaxed shoulders

The clarinet produces the sound by the player pushing a constant stream of air through the instrument known as the 'air stream' or the 'air column'.

To inhale sufficient air to play, and to be able to control that air, it's imperative to work with a straight back and relaxed shoulders, whether sitting or standing. Beginners often neglect to keep the back straight, so it is wise to get into the habit of addressing good posture, every single time before playing commences. By maintaining the straight back, upright torso natural position, you can take air into the bottom of the lungs and control it as it is pushed through the clarinet to produce the best performance.

Sitting or standing?

Teachers have specific preferences as to whether their students sit or stand to play. You will develop your own preference in time. It is easier to enable students to obtain a better sound if they are standing because their body shape is natural, they breathe well, and they do not have to think much about their posture.

When a student is young and not fully-grown, it is often a challenge to stand all the time as the clarinet can become heavy. I suggest that you make this the rule – **you can choose to either sit or stand to play, however you MUST promise yourself, and continuously remind yourself, to keep your back upright.** It makes no difference whether you sit or stand to play, providing the back is straight.

A 'Straight Back' Exercise

Do this please

- Stand straight, with your feet slightly apart, your shoulders relaxed and with a chair behind your legs. Sense the feeling of your straight back.

- Without moving your back, bend your knees and sit down keeping the feet flat and anchored on the floor.
- Notice the three right angles that you have created – at the ankle, between the feet and the lower half of the legs, at the knee, between the lower and upper halves of the legs and most importantly at the base of the spine between the top half of the leg and the back. Sense that your torso is in the same position as when you were standing.

Smile – you have achieved a perfect playing position! From here you will be able to control the air from the diaphragm muscle below the lungs.

Do not sit like a banana!

Collapsing the base of the spine is not good for playing. I call this 'sitting like a banana' as the back and the legs form one continuous curve. This position may be OK for watching television eating a pizza but it's no good for clarinet playing. It squashes the bottom of the lungs, prevents them filling to capacity and produces a weak and unfocused sound.

Three steps to '**The Best Sitting to Play Position**'

1. Put the feet flat firmly on the floor, slightly apart.
2. Sit upright from the base of the spine.
3. Fully relax the shoulders.

It is not enough to simply think 'sit up straight' as this thought may encourage you to lift your shoulders too. Give your whole focus to the feeling of the base of the spine in your back and sit up from there, and you will create a strong playing position which feels good.

About Air Control

The skill of pushing out a controlled column of air through the clarinet is one of the top fundamental skills of playing!

The diaphragm is the muscle used to push the air through the clarinet. There are so many things to focus on at the beginning of learning and it is unnecessary to go into elaborate detail about diaphragm control here. It is, however, wise to gain a brief overview of this muscle and to be aware that you will aim to use it as the weeks go by.

The diaphragm is a dome-shaped fibrous sheet underneath the lungs. From the moment we are born, it works every time we take a breath in and every time we breathe out. When air enters the body, the diaphragm contracts, going down to a flat shape to allow the lungs to expand. When the air is expired, it elevates and resumes the dome shape.

Identifying many of the muscles in the body is easy. If we pump up our arm, we can feel the pronounced muscle, and we identify with its shape. The diaphragm muscle is less easy to sense inside the body. We have breathed automatically since birth, and probably have never had a reason to consider the breath, never mind be asked to control it with the diaphragm. The exercise 'Diaphragm Discovery' below will give you the first sense of this muscle, but please be aware that players develop increased awareness and sensitivity to it over time and not necessarily on the first day of playing.

Four Vital Breathing Exercises

For these exercises, you will not need your clarinet. Do them in sequence, and be sure not to skip any of them. They will engage you completely as you identify with the sensory feeling of breathing in and out, just as you will with the instrument later.

Exercise 1 'Just Imagine'

The air is around us all the time. We never think about it. We take it for granted, but we instinctively know that it is there and that there is enough for every breath that we take for the rest of our life.

We can't see this air – but we CAN **imagine a shape of air.**

Do this please

- Imagine the shape of a tall column. Make a picture of this in your mind. This column goes from the ground right up to the very top of a high ceiling, the kind you may get in a large Roman temple that is holding up the roof.
- Picture the even round circumference and the sides of the column, which are perfectly smooth and polished right to the top.

- Now imagine another shape. This time, it's something you might eat. I want you to imagine a sausage, a very long sausage. This sausage is even with smooth sides.

When we push air through the clarinet, we imagine we are driving the 'shape' of a long even sausage, or the 'shape' of a tall even column of air, right down to the very end of the clarinet.

Exercise 2 'A Feel Good Toooooo'

Do this please

- Take a breath in as if you were going to sing a note.
- Say a big, long 'Toooooo' sound as you push the air out forcefully. Keep it going for as long as you can, as if you were playing a sustained note on the clarinet.
- Imagine driving the shape of a sausage of air through to the lowest part of the clarinet.
- Do this a few times, keeping the shoulders relaxed and down. Make sure the air you push out is forceful and even, not shaky – wobbly sausages of air make wobbly sounds.
- Check out you have an inner sense of being totally relaxed. Although you will drive the long 'Toooooo' out with some energy and speed, imagine you are making a long and relaxed sigh and feel fully alert and comfortable as you do so.

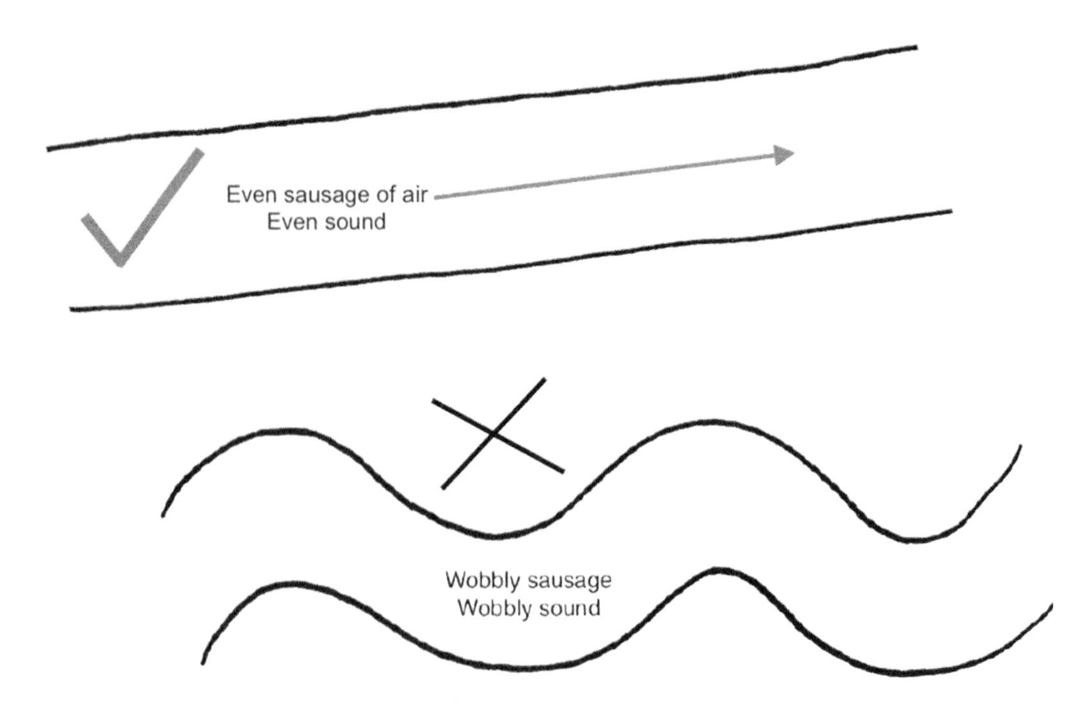

By imagining the even column/sausage of air travelling directly from the bottom of the lungs, up through the relaxed, open throat and down to the very end of the clarinet bell, you will start to get an idea, and **develop an awareness of controlling the air** as you push it out. Most of the air, of course, does not reach the bottom of the instrument as it comes out of the holes that are open. However, by 'imagining' the shape of the air column traveling down to the bell you will begin to experience the smooth passage of air through the instrument, and you will be well on the way to making a great sound.

Do the same exercise but this time imagine you are blowing out a candle. Follow the steps.

Do this please

- Focus on the shoulder blades in the back, underneath the neck. Keeping the shoulders relaxed and low, pull the shoulder blades backward as if you want them to meet. Notice how you have opened and expanded the chest cavity.
- Put one hand flat firmly on your stomach just above your waist.
- Put the other arm out at arms-length with the open palm towards you.
- Breathe in with lots of energy through the mouth. Take a long deep breath into the bottom of the lungs.
- **Forcefully push out the air** as if you are blowing out a candle a long way from your face. 'Toooooo'. **Feel the strong movement in your stomach area** as you **keep the air going** to 'blow out the candle'. By directing the air you will feel it in your open palm.

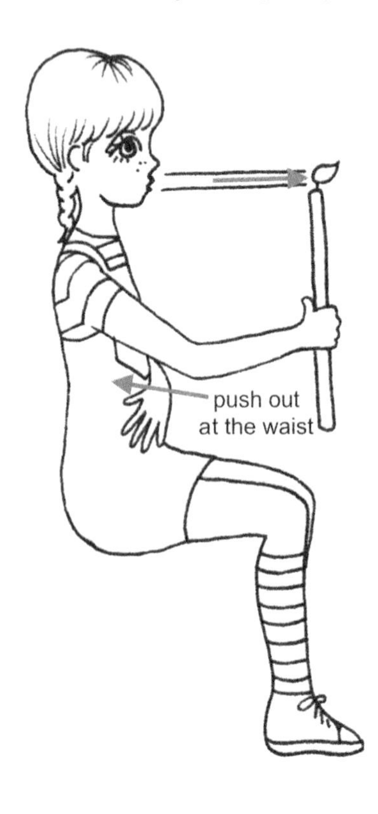

Exercise 3 'Low Down Shoulders'

When you ask someone to take a big breath they usually lift their shoulders as high as they can, take in as much air as possible into the top part of the lungs, and look as though they will pop. This kind of breathing is simply no good for clarinet playing! The bottom of the lungs must be filled with air when inhaling.

How are YOU breathing? Check you are filling the lower part of the lungs and not lifting your shoulders as you inhale.

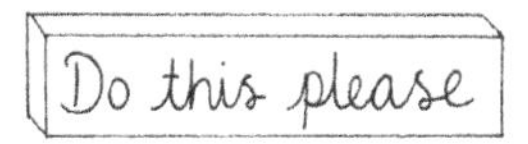

- Stand in front of a mirror.
- Rest the flat palm of one hand on your chest.
- Place the other palm firmly on your abdomen, just underneath the ribs.
- Take a breath in and notice what happens.

If the lower hand moved, you are taking air into the bottom part of your lungs and keeping the shoulders down – well done!

If the top hand moved, you are raising your shoulders.

Practise this exercise a few times till you get the idea and automatically take the air into the bottom part of the lungs whilst keeping the shoulders low and relaxed. You may like to imagine you are breathing in to make a big sigh as you inhale.

Do not get hung up on this exercise. If you are not getting it quite right now, that's fine – move on. Breathing skills, as with many other skills, develop over time and you will be able to take air into the bottom of your lungs very soon, once you get going.

Exercise 4 'Diaphragm Discovery'

This exercise will help you to feel the diaphragm muscle which you will use to control the air column over time. See how you get on.

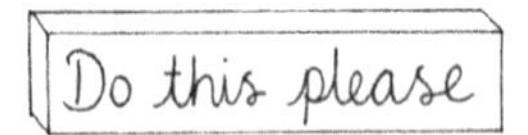

- Sit or stand with a straight back.
- Lay the palms of your hands firmly on the sides of your abdomen at waist height, fingers pointing to the front, thumbs pointing to the back.
- Breathe in as if you were going to sing a song.
- Push out your hands at the waist from your abdomen as you forcefully say a long 'Toooooo'.
- Feel the movement from your waist in your fingers and thumbs at the back. This is your diaphragm working.

As with all muscles the diaphragm strength and control develops with time and practice.

The magic word is 'THROUGH'.
We push the air THROUGH the clarinet.
We do not 'blow' into it as if blowing up a balloon.

Command of the air develops over time, not necessarily from day one of playing. It is continuously worked on by musicians in all stages of expertise as they strive to produce the best possible sound on every occasion.

Be aware of air control from the very beginning.
It is a fundamental skill –
one we need today and every single time we play.

Sensible Sling Use

Usually, the right thumb takes the weight of the clarinet. For the first period of playing, the thumb may find it a challenge to support the instrument. Many players, especially young ones with small hands, get a red thumb which can get sore and uncomfortable, then the hand will twist round the clarinet, making it difficult to use the fingers correctly.

In the last few years, the use of a sling has become popular for new players. Many instruments, specially made for beginners, now have a ring on top of the thumb rest to cater for the hook of the sling. The primary purpose of the sling is to take the weight of the clarinet off the thumb and put it on the neck. The relieved thumb then sits underneath the thumb rest and merely guides the instrument into playing the position.

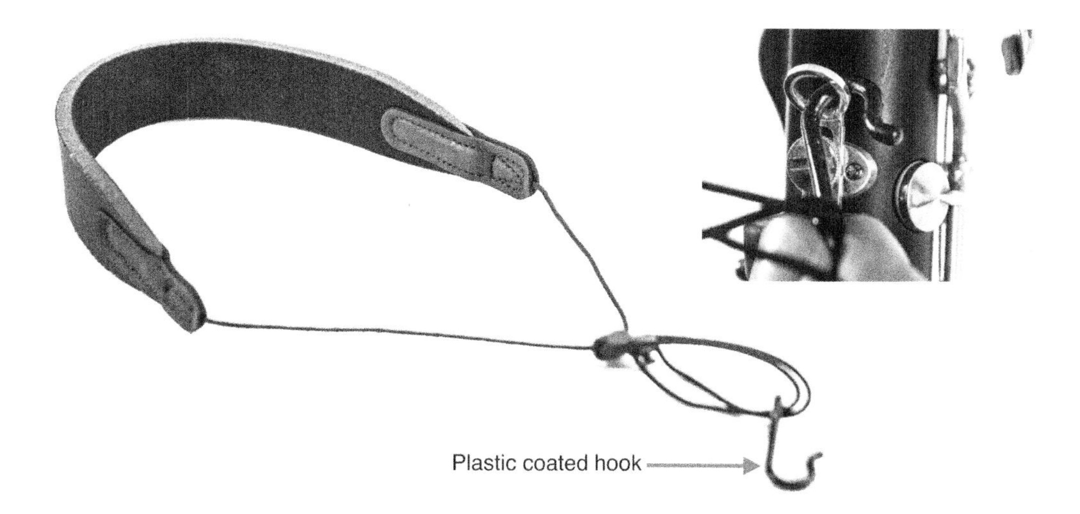

After a period, when players feel accustomed to handling the clarinet, they usually abandon the sling because there is much more freedom of movement and expression when playing without it.

If you choose to use a sling, note that the productive and comfortable use of it depends on two important factors:

1. The position of the neckpiece on the neck.
2. The length of the sling.

Given these considerations, the sling will enhance your playing experience considerably.

The perfect length for the sling is that which enables the player to put the clarinet in the mouth without moving the head and neck, which should remain in a relaxed, neutral position to play.

When the sling is too long, the player stretches the neck to get the mouthpiece in the mouth.

When the sling is too short, the player will push the head backward to get the mouthpiece in the mouth.

Having a sling that is too short or too long is simply no good. It results in a strained neck, a tense embouchure (mouth position) and a poor sound and feels jolly uncomfortable! When the head is in the neutral position and the clarinet is held away from the body the best sounds are made.

How to use the sling

Develop the habit of giving special attention to the sling every single time you prepare to play.

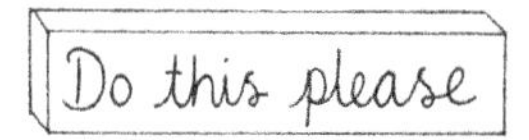

- Place the sling over the head and put the neckpiece as low down as possible to avoid straining the neck.
- Make sure the neckpiece is over the clothing. Having it directly on the bare skin is less comfortable as it could dig into the skin over a long period of playing.
- Place the hook of the sling through the ring on the thumb rest on the back of the clarinet.
- Adjust the length of the sling to where it provides the most comfort so you can put the mouthpiece in the mouth without moving the neck.

- When taking the sling off try to keep it at the length you are working with, then you don't have to reset it the next time you play.
- If your clarinet doesn't have a ring, approach a repair specialist who will quickly change the thumb rest and replace it with one with an attached ring.

  OR

- Use a rubber thumb rest. If you are not using a sling your right-hand thumb will feel more comfortable using a rubber rest which is usually thicker and softer than the cork, underneath the rest. Once the rubber rest is in place, it will stay there tightly. Don't take it on and off, as this will slacken the opening in the rubber and it will ping off easily.

OR

- Make sure that the underside of the thumb rest has either a piece of cork or felt to cushion your thumb.

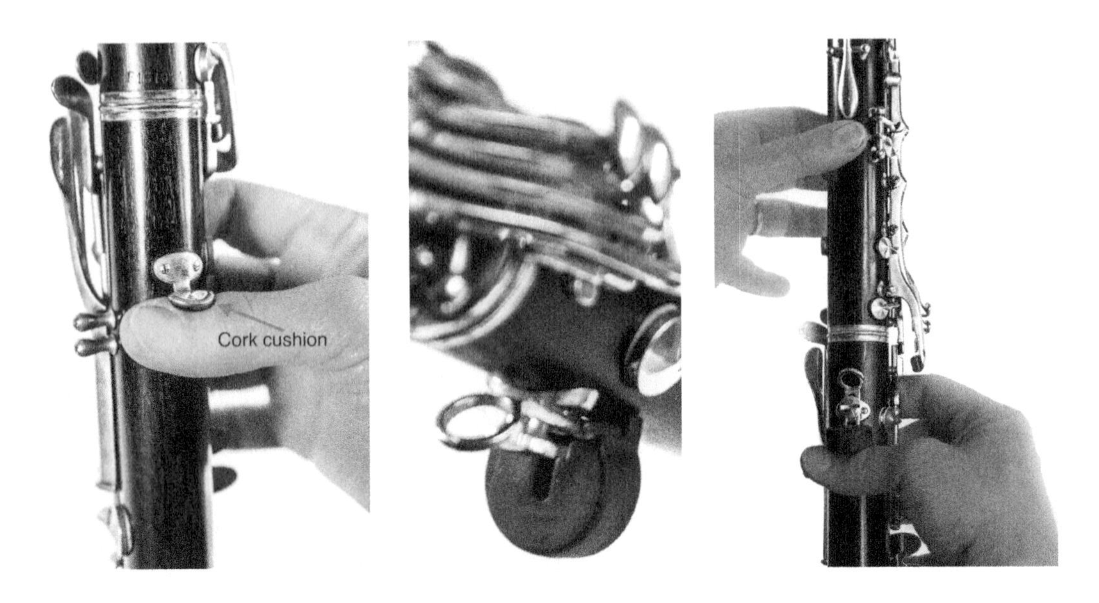

A VERY important piece of advice for sling users

Take extra special care to hold the clarinet out, away from your body, when playing with the sling. Because the weight of the instrument is taken by the sling around the neck there is always a temptation for beginners to allow the clarinet to drop near the body which is not a good position to play from.

Let's Get Hands-On

As you read this section visualise your left hand at the top of the clarinet and the right hand at the bottom.

The placing of the hands and fingers on the instrument has an enormous impact on the ease of playing and the ability to develop an efficient technique.

Usually, in the first few lessons, beginners give all their focus to the fingers of the left hand, at the top of the clarinet, as it's easier to produce the notes in that area of the instrument. The only thought they give to the right hand is to put the thumb underneath the thumb rest, and then the fingers of that hand often get neglected. After a while, when it's necessary to use the right hand, those fingers are habitually stuck in uncomfortable positions and find it hard to work fluently. So, it's important to pay attention to *both* hands from the outset.

Give their positions equal consideration in each practice session, even though the fingers of the right hand may be used less in the first few weeks. By establishing helpful habits, we avoid practising in unhelpful habits that can slow down the technique and impair development.

Clarinets are built perfectly to fit the shape of our hands

The holes that we cover and the keys that we press are all in their specific positions to make the hands and fingers feel comfortable and allow them to work smoothly.

The best way to put the hands on to the clarinet is in a natural way, just as they are, without bending them in any way.

Look at your hand and arm, and move the fingers a little. The ligaments and bones connect the fingers, hand, and arm. Notice the movement of the ligaments in the arm when the fingers gently move. By keeping a natural, relaxed position in the arm, hands and wrist, the fingers work freely.

Whether you are right or left handed, the Right Hand operates the bottom half of the instrument and the Left Hand operates the top.

The 'Hands-On' Exercise

Feel how relaxed the hands are when they keep their natural positions.

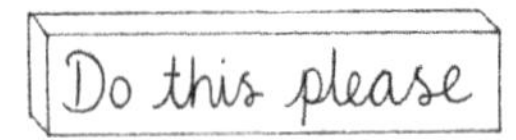

- Hold the assembled clarinet with the left hand. Put the bell on the knee and rest the top of the clarinet on the left shoulder. Keep the mouthpiece cap on to protect the reed.
- Relax your right hand by your side. Shake the wrist a little.
- Lift the hand and see the shape of the thumb and fingers. They should look like a letter 'C' facing backward.

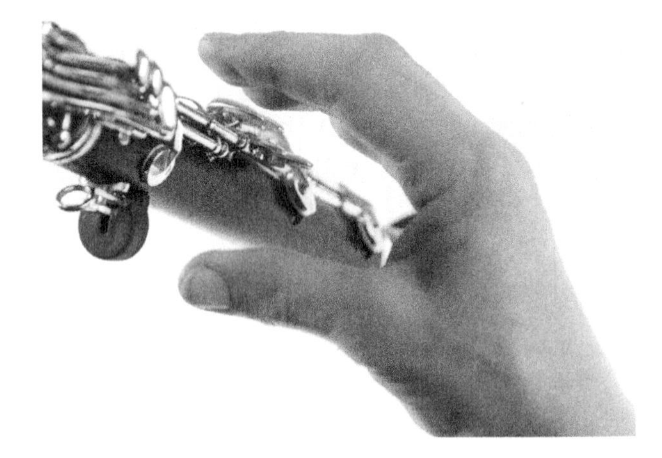

- Keep this form and slot it into the bottom joint, placing the straight thumb underneath the thumb rest. Place the thumb rest between the nail and the knuckle of the thumb.
- Place the pads of the first three fingers on the first three holes. Cover them entirely if you can, and press the ring keys that go around them. If you cannot cover the holes completely, no problem, just do the best you can for now. Notice how all your fingers feel on this joint.
- Use the fourth finger on the four keys at the bottom. Play around pressing them and move from key to key.

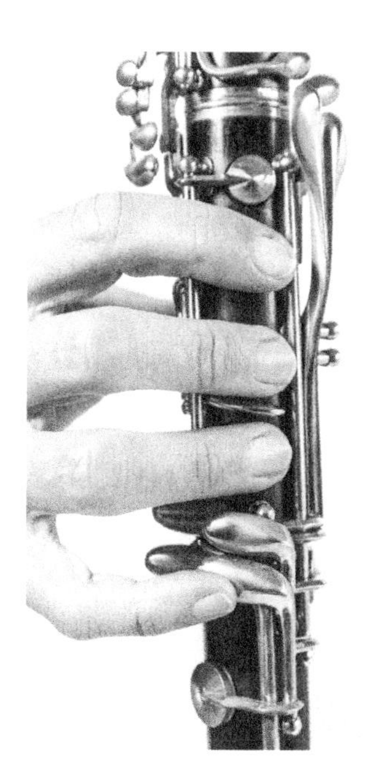

- Make sure the first finger is not touching the long side key on the upper joint.

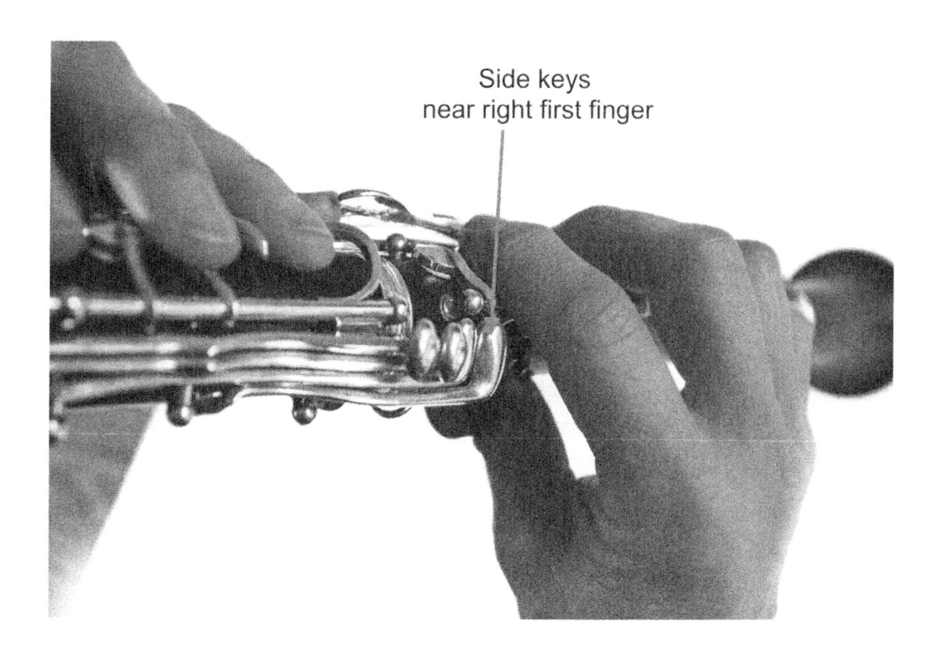

- Drop the left hand by your side. Shake the relaxed wrist.
- Lift the hand and see its natural position. This time the thumb and first finger make a 'C' position, the right way around.

- Keep this position and slot the hand into the top joint. Cover the thumb hole, pressing the ring key around it.

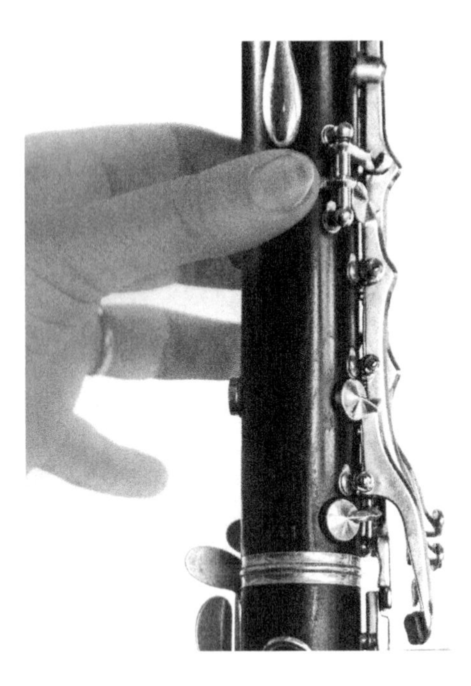

- Cover the three holes with the pads of the first three fingers, again taking care to push the ring keys down that go around the two top holes.
- Use the fourth finger – the little one – to play around with the four keys nearby.

- Take time to appreciate that you are keeping both hands away from the side keys of the instrument.

For the first few weeks, do the above exercise, before the start of playing! Give attention to experiencing and appreciating the tactile feeling of the positions of the hands on the clarinet to develop strong habitual hand positions. Do not barge into playing without doing this exercise, or the right hand will get stuck grasping the clarinet at the bottom. By focusing on both hands from the very beginning, you will find your finger technique developing quickly.

Make sure that:

- All the knuckles of the fingers are slightly bent, and the hands are in an arched shape.
- The fingers do not go too far over the holes, and the pads of the fingers are used to cover them.
- The middle fingers are, more or less, at right angles to the clarinet. This will prevent the sides of both first fingers touching the nearby keys.

Having both hands in a natural, relaxed position gives great balance to the clarinet when the fingers move.

It doesn't matter how many fingers come off, the hands stay in the same place so the clarinet is balanced and will not shake.

It's OK for fully-grown adults!

It's easy for adults to reach all the keys and to cover the holes completely with their fully-grown hands but if you are a very young beginner, you may struggle to stretch to the keys as I have asked you to do. Please do not worry. As you grow, it will become easier. Now it is important to be aware of the hand positions that you aim for. Keep having a go, appreciate the feeling of the fingers on the keys and enjoy your progress as you move towards your target.

Clarinet Angle

The angle at which the mouthpiece is in the mouth has a huge impact on the sound quality, and on how easy it is to get the sound. Rather than focusing on the mouthpiece, think about the angle of the whole instrument. By holding the clarinet out at an approximate angle of 40° or slightly less, from the body, the air will go through the gap between the reed and the mouthpiece and allow the reed to vibrate freely.

Never allow the clarinet to be too close to your body as the reed will squash against the mouthpiece then you might force the air and make a small sound, or maybe no sound will come out at all. Holding the clarinet too far away is also not a good idea because this will make the sound unfocused and you may squeak.

Consider your arms:

- If the sides of your arms are touching your body, the clarinet is too low.
- If they lift from their sockets, they will get tired. This position is unnecessary, and you may look like a bird about to fly.
- If your arms and shoulders are relaxed and your elbows are slightly pushed forward of the body you may have achieved the perfect angle at which to produce your best sound. Well done!

Watch your free online course
'**Clarinet Kickstart**' for extra support with this chapter
visit www.ClarinetBeginnersCourse.co.uk

How to Use a Music Stand

Most times, we just take the music stand for granted because we accept it as a convenient music prop, assembling it any old how and using it without much thought.

However, by considering both the height of the music stand and the distance from the body, we can enhance our primary objectives, that of making the best quality sound and making the sound production easy!

Of course, the best height and distance are those that enable the player to feel relaxed while producing the best sound possible. When the head and neck are in a natural position, these positive results can be achieved with more ease.

The distance between the stand and the body:

- If your music stand is too close, you may be forced to have the clarinet too low near your body, squashing the reed to the mouthpiece and making it difficult to produce a full, open tone.
- Put your music stand at a distance that allows you to hold the clarinet out from your body.
- Check that you can hold the clarinet at the best angle without it touching the stand.

The height of the music stand:

- Put the top of your music stand at a height that enables you to keep your head in a neutral position.
- Hold the clarinet in place and put it in your mouth. Check that you can see the music and glance up without moving your head up and down, imagining you are looking up at the conductor of your band.

When a stand is either too high or too low, the player constantly looks up and down to see the music, with the clarinet in the mouth. This disturbs the mouth position and the pitch of the note in the process.

If you look up to a stand which is far too high, you will tilt your head upward, press the reed to the mouthpiece, and make a small closed sound. If you look down to a music stand that is far too low, you will tilt your head downwards altering the angle of the mouthpiece in the mouth considerably. Your top teeth may slide down the mouthpiece beak, and invariably this will lead to squeaks. Whether sitting or standing, I would recommend that you play with the top of the music stand somewhere around chin height.

No music stand? No problem!

Lots of beginners don't possess a stand at the beginning of learning. Nevertheless, keep the music height and distance in mind when you are playing from a music sheet. Use a pile of books to prop the music to the best height.

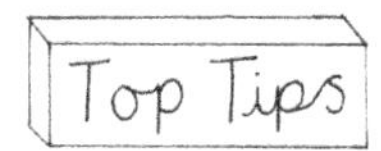

- When performing at a concert or taking an exam, never hide behind the music stand – your audience wants to see you as well as hear you.
- Do not take examples of players you see on the television who have their stands in all sorts of places or who are waving their clarinets around to play. They are professional players with established mouth positions who have been playing for some time. Please follow the above advice until you develop stable mature sounds and playing habits.

How to assemble a traditional fold-up stand

Music stands are easy to bend. Keep your cool and avoid getting into a tangle with these simple steps.

To open the stand:

- Pivot the top of the stand into an almost upright position and secure with the screw.
- Open out four arms – one long and one short on each side. The long arms form the top and sides of the stand. The short arm forms the inner diagonal support.
- Point the long arms upwards towards the ceiling and point the short arms downwards.

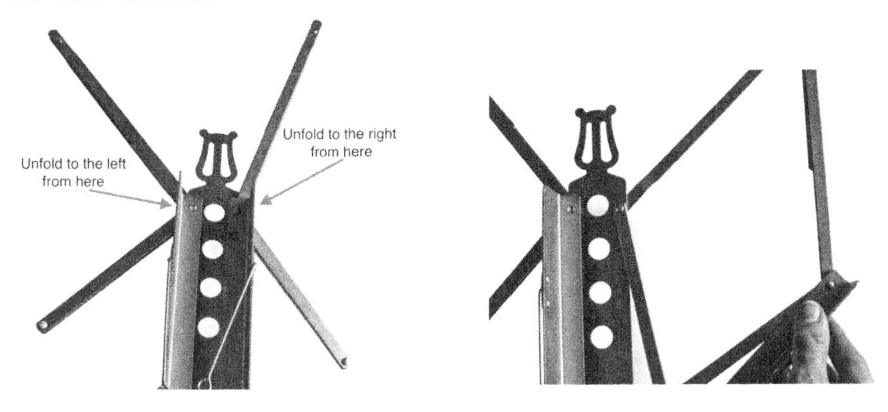

- From the point where the long and short arms pivot together, unfold one side of the stand at a time, gently prising the lower arm into place in the middle of the music stand and the longer arm to form the outer rim.
- Open the legs of the stand and adjust the height.

To fold the stand:

- Folding each half, in turn, press the join of the inner arm, in the middle of the stand, downwards. This small arm will fold inwards, and the outside of the stand will fold upwards forming the long arm.
- Fold the long arm down to the side to meet the short arm and fold up the legs.

Rooted Like a Tree

Having a great posture when standing to play will give you tremendous confidence. We have already learned about the importance of keeping the back straight and having relaxed shoulders and arms when playing. Add to these essential things a feeling of stability and security as you stand, being anchored to the ground, and you will be ready to perform on stage in no time.

Standing with your feet together is an unstable position for playing and will not add to your confidence. That's almost like standing on one leg like a stork!

Having your feet about 15 - 20 cm apart will anchor you securely to the stage!

You can help yourself to feel confident by the way you think. Imagine all your weight going into your feet and imagine yourself as a tall tree with strong roots. Your roots spread broad and deep down into the earth from both your anchored feet. Feeling like an anchored tree, there is nothing that can rock you. You feel sturdy and centred and ready to perform. You will be amazed at how much air you can take into the lower part of the lungs, how efficiently you can control the air, and how confident you feel from your stable position.

Incidentally, using your imagination in this way is jolly useful whenever you take a playing exam, speak in public, present yourself for an interview, or on any occasion when you may feel slightly nervous.

Feel confident and satisfied that you will deliver an incredible performance!

All Together Now

Keep your playing on track by nurturing helpful habits and checking you are practising all you have learned in this chapter. Always handle your instrument well and play with the best posture and breathing skills.

Helpful habits get you what you want! You are working towards 'The Best Sound in Town', our next chapter!

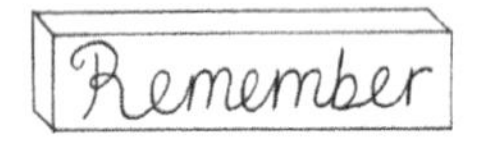

- Sit/stand with a straight back and relaxed shoulders.
- Adjust the sling to the perfect length so the head can remain in a neutral position.
- Put the natural position of the hands on the clarinet without distorting them.
- Use the pads of the fingers to cover the holes of the clarinet and keep the sides of the first fingers away from the side keys of the clarinet.
- Hold the clarinet out, away from the body at a suitable angle so the arms are not touching the sides and the air can travel through the mouthpiece.
- Open the chest to take as much air into the lungs as needed.
- Breathe from the lower part of the lungs.
- Control the sound by pushing an even column of air through the clarinet.
- Place the music stand far enough away from the body so you can hold the clarinet out.
- Have the top of the music stand just around chin height so that you can see both the music and the conductor without moving the head.
- Stand to play with confidence and stability, rooting yourself to the ground.

Your good habits get you on track before you play!

CHAPTER 3

The Best Sound in Town

- It's All About the Sound
- What is the Embouchure?
- The Muscles of the Mouth
- Steps for Making the Sound
- Exercise 'Quick Sound Instruction'
- Exercise 'Six Steps to Easy Embouchure and Sound'
- Extra Embouchure Explanation – Are You Smiling?
- The Best Tone Exercise
- A Sound Summary

It's All About the Sound

Do you know the kind of sound that you are aiming for? The clarinet's principal attraction is the amazing sound that it makes. You will have listened to the instrument countless times and love its tone. Imagine that sound in your mind. Can you hear it? We all possess a 'mind's eye' where we can see a picture in our imagination, especially if we close our eyes. In the same way, we can also hear a sound in our head.

Be an excellent listener. All musicians need good listening skills, so let's draw our attention to developing them right at the very beginning. Players listen acutely to their playing so they can continuously modify and produce their best sound. They also listen to the musicians they are playing with to ensure they're playing in tune and blending with them.

Good listening skills can enhance your daily experience as you become receptive to the live sounds around you. Develop your basic skills by becoming aware and alert to everything you hear. Be discerning about the sound qualities you prefer and that resonate with you, and you will be surprised at the detail you hear. There is music round every corner – and that perceived as noise by someone else may be music to your ears.

Listen to good clarinet playing as much as you can, in whatever environment you can, on the television, in concerts, buskers on street corners and online.

As you read this chapter on sound production, be aware of the tonality in your inner ear that you aim for.

It's all about the sound!

What is the Embouchure?

When clarinet players talk about the embouchure, they are referring to the shape of the mouth when playing. It's almost a buzzword with players. You will come across it time and time again. Teachers and players constantly talk about strengthening the embouchure, the embouchure position, adjusting the embouchure, a relaxed embouchure, and so on. The focus on the embouchure never ends. A good teacher and a vigilant player will always be on the lookout trying to improve and strengthen it because it can enhance the sound considerably.

In French, the words 'la bouche' means the mouth, and in music the word 'embouchure' refers to the formation of the mouth to play a wind instrument. Embouchure is the combination of the lips, teeth, tongue, mouth size and cavity, and the slackness or tension of the cheek walls.

Though this may sound rather complicated, beginners think of embouchure as how and where the teeth and lips are around the mouthpiece.

A sensitive and reliable embouchure develops over a period – not on the first day of playing! It is worked on continuously through a player's experience. It becomes pleasurable and exciting to develop as the sound blossoms more and more, as the embouchure strength and control evolves.

Do not get hung up on your embouchure if, in the beginning, you find that making the sound is not as simple as you may have imagined. Follow the necessary steps, exercise some patience and eventually, you will make a good sound – that's a promise!

The Muscles of the Mouth

The face and head have an impressive set of interlinking, elastic and flexible muscles which are attached to the skin – there are about 47 in all.

The massive, thick circular muscle around the mouth connects to the grimace muscle, the nose muscle, the cheek muscles and the muscles in the chin. These all work in conjunction to enable us to chew our food and make all our facial expressions – and they are essential when it comes to clarinet playing too!

It is the clarinetist's aim to use these muscles to help control the reed and mouthpiece to make the best sound possible.

The muscles involved primarily for clarinet playing are the chin muscles which go in a vertical direction and the circular muscle around the mouth, which is named the Orbicularis Oris. You do not need to remember its name but be aware that you are using this muscle as you play.

Many people play perfectly well without ever giving any thought or consideration to their facial muscles, or that they are even using them at all, but by being aware of the face muscles you will appreciate why it's important to do frequent practice. In the beginning, the muscles of the mouth have never been used in the same way as they are when playing the clarinet. They are not strong and toned and can soon feel achy after playing for a while. We exercise our bodies to keep the muscles toned and conditioned. In the same way, with regular practising, we can exercise the embouchure muscles to enable them to control the reed and enhance the sound.

Regular bursts of short, concentrated practice each day will tone and strengthen the muscles very quickly, enabling you to play for some considerable time. Practising for an hour, once a week, the night before the lesson, will have little benefit, as the untoned muscles of the mouth will not be able to cope. You will end up biting the mouthpiece, making a tight sound and your lips will feel exhausted.

The First Sound

There is no right or wrong way to make the sound. The best way for any player is that which produces the most pleasant tone and feels sustainable and comfortable. Some beginners instantly put the clarinet in their mouth and produce a good sound without much instruction, however, these people are extremely few and far between. Most players need guidance and gently coaxing along the way.

A standard method of sound production has evolved over the years that has been adopted by the majority. This process of making the sound is described here in various ways for your understanding.

Read through the exercise 'Steps for Making the Sound' to get a general understanding of the process, then play along as you follow the two exercises 'Quick Sound Instruction' and 'Six Steps to Easy Embouchure and Sound.'

Reading exercise:

Steps for Making the Sound

If you feel these instructions are rather detailed, don't be alarmed – everything is made simple for you in the following playing exercises:

- Turn a little bottom lip over the lower teeth. Stretch it to the sides creating a 'cushion' for the reed.
- Place the mouthpiece 1 cm into the mouth, with the reed facing downwards and resting on the lower lip. Apply a slight downward pressure to anchor the reed to the lip.
- Put the top teeth securely on the top of the mouthpiece. Do not bite.
- Close the lips around the mouthpiece.
- Make a slight 'smile' at the mouth corners. This prevents the cheeks puffing out when the air passes through the clarinet.
- Keeping the bottom lip and top teeth in place breathe in through the sides of the mouth.
- Place the tip of the tongue just under the tip of the reed.
- As you push the air through the gap between the reed and the mouthpiece, strike the reed with the tongue to start the sound, as if pronouncing the sound 'Taaaaaaaaa'.

Now for Some Playing!

Before we begin, please understand that some people get the sound straight away and others take a while. Whatever happens with you is perfectly ok because you will make a lovely sound eventually. Just don't expect too much at first. With most beginners, it takes time, practice and patience.

Keep relaxed and enjoy each stage of learning. As you become more familiar with the feeling of the clarinet in the mouth, your sound will start to evolve and develop.

Playing exercise 1:

Quick Sound Instruction

The 'Quick Sound Instruction' exercise uses the whole of the assembled instrument. This exercise is quick and easy, and can be gratifying if the sound comes out immediately:

- Assemble the clarinet and moisten the reed.
- Stand to play if possible and keep the back straight and shoulders relaxed. If you need to sit do not rest the bell on your knee.
- Put the right thumb underneath the thumb rest in between the nail and the knuckle.
- Hold the barrel with the left hand.
- Push the clarinet 40° away from your body.
- Put the lips naturally together then put the tip of the mouthpiece in the lips with the reed downwards.
- Slowly push the mouthpiece into the mouth so the lower lip draws over the bottom teeth and the top teeth are on the top of the mouthpiece. GENTLY push air into the mouthpiece as you SLOWLY push the clarinet into the mouth to make the sound. You will find the exact place where the sound is made.
- Practise this till you achieve the sound every time.

Special points:

- The cheeks do not puff out – avoid this by making a slight 'smile' at the mouth corners.
- The reed anchors to the bottom lip.
- The top teeth rest firmly on the beak of the mouthpiece.
- The mouthpiece goes to you – do not stretch your neck to get it into your mouth.

Playing exercise 2:

Six Steps to Easy Embouchure and Sound

The 'Six Steps to Easy Embouchure and Sound' exercise simplifies the process of sound production to ensure that your mouth position, breathing and articulation skills are all tip top. For this exercise, at first use the first finger then the mouthpiece and barrel together, without the rest of the instrument. This will enable you to fully focus on each small task in turn without having to deal with the weight of the clarinet at the same time.

As well as embouchure formation and sound production, this exercise teaches **two essential fundamental skills** of playing:

- **Breathing in and out of the mouth (the nose is NEVER involved in playing).**
- **Using the tongue to articulate the reed to make a good start to the notes.**

Once you become familiar with these skill sets, you will feel relaxed and comfortable producing your sound.

Learn these simple steps in sequence. Take your time. Only move on when you feel satisfied you have mastered the point of each step. Each small section builds on the previous one and the previous steps are repeated in small print for your extra support should you need it.

You will need three things:

1. A hand mirror – you need to LOOK as well as LISTEN.
2. The barrel and the mouthpiece together – with a moist reed secured by the ligature. A suitable strength reed for a beginner is 1½.
3. The main body of the clarinet assembled.

Place the mirror near you at head height, so you can look straight across at yourself without putting your head either down or up.

If you haven't got a hand mirror, stand near a wall mirror to do the exercises.

No mirror at all? Ask someone to watch and check you are doing the exercises correctly. There is absolutely no point in guessing. In fact, it can be extremely handy to have someone read the instructions for you, as you do the exercises.

Have fun with these – you'll be making a great sound by the end!

Step 1

FOCUS ON: The bottom lip

Focus on the feeling of the lower lip as it turns and stretches over the lower teeth.

Use the first finger. Pretend that the finger is the mouthpiece:

- Turn a small part of the lower lip over the lower teeth.
- Stretch the lip to the sides. Imagine you are applying lip balm on a cold day. Notice that it is the muscle in the lip that is stretching.
- LOOK in the mirror. See the **pink part of the lip over your teeth**. If you can see skin over your teeth, you have put too much face into your mouth!
- Put the tip of the finger in the middle of the pink lip imagining that this is the mouthpiece. Roll the finger on the lip and press gently. Feel the teeth underneath the finger. Keep it at about a 40° angle to the body.
- LOOK in the mirror and make sure:
    - Your finger is resting in the *middle* of the lip.
    - You see the *pink* part of your lip at either side of the finger.
    - Your lip is *stretched* to the sides.
- Put the top teeth down onto the top of the finger. Be firm but do not bite.
- Close the gap around the finger with the sides of the mouth.
- Make a slight 'smile' at the mouth corners.

Watch the module on
Sound Production
in your free online course
'Clarinet Kickstart'

Step 2

FOCUS ON: Breathing IN through the mouth

Focus on breathing IN through the sides of the mouth without involving the nose. The nose is NEVER involved in clarinet playing.

Use the first finger.

As before:

- Stretch the pink part of the lower lip over the teeth.
- Rest your first finger at a 40° angle in the centre.
- Put the top teeth firmly on to the finger.
- Make a slight 'smile' at the mouth corners.

- Keep the top teeth and lower lip in place, relax the lips and breathe in slowly through the sides of the mouth.
- Breathe out slowly through the sides of the mouth.
- Practise over and over. Keep the lips relaxed to allow the air to come in and out of the sides of the mouth. Do not puff the cheeks. Keep the tiny smile.

- LOOK in the mirror and make sure:
  - Your lips are relaxed.
  - The top teeth and lower lip stay in place as you breathe in.
  - You breathe in through the sides of the mouth.
  - You are not puffing the cheeks out. If you are, make a better 'smile' at the mouth corners as the air goes out.

Step 3

FOCUS ON: Breathing OUT through the mouthpiece

Focus on the feeling of the movement of the air as it travels through the mouthpiece.

Listen for the air as you breathe as naturally as possible with only a little more effort than normal and make the quietest sound you can, like the wind on a mild day.

Use the mouthpiece and barrel together.

Look at the mouthpiece from the side. Note the place where the curve of the mouthpiece opening bends away from the reed. This place is where the reed rests on the lip.

Like before:

- Turn the pink part of the lip over the teeth, stretching it to the sides.
- Anchor the reed to the centre of the lip by pressing it gently.
- Put the top teeth firmly on the top of the mouthpiece.
- Keeping the top teeth and bottom lip in place, breathe in through the sides of the mouth.

- Close the lips around the mouthpiece and push the air gently through the gap 'Hooooooooooooo' – for as long as you can. Keep the 'smile' at the mouth corners.
- Repeat – breathe in through the sides of the mouth – out through the mouthpiece – in through the sides of the mouth – out through the mouthpiece. If you squeak, push the air more gently. If you can't get the air through the mouthpiece, stop biting!

- LOOK in the mirror and make sure:
  - Your lips are flexible and relaxed so they allow the air to come in through the sides of the mouth.
  - They seal around the mouthpiece so all the air travels through it and does not escape from the sides of the mouth.

Step 4

FOCUS ON: An EVEN air column

Focus on the feeling of pushing the air a little harder through the mouthpiece to make an even sound.

Use the mouthpiece and barrel together for this step. You might think you sound like a duck with this step and cry with laughter. The mouthpiece and barrel alone will never make a fantastic sound – but make the best sound you can for now.

It will be obvious if you push out an even sausage of air or a wobbly one. Ask yourself, 'am I making my best sound?' and 'is my sound even and smooth?', then you will start to exercise one of the most important rules of playing – listening to the quality of the sound all the time!

As before:

- Turn the pink part of the lip over the teeth, stretching it to the sides.
- Anchor the reed to the centre of the lip by pressing it gently. Keep at 40° to the body.
- Put the top teeth firmly on to the top of the mouthpiece.
- Breathe in through the sides of the mouth.

- Push the air firmly through the mouthpiece. Keep it going and make a big sound. You need to blow a little harder and faster than you did in the previous exercise when you were just listening for the sound of the air.
- Repeat – relax the sides of the mouth (while maintaining the top teeth and bottom lip in their place). Breathe in. Close the lips around the sides and push the air through the mouthpiece again. Imagine the shape of an even sausage of air – 'Hoooooooooo'.

Check that you are not bunching the lower lip upwards towards the reed. Make sure you keep a 'flat' appearance of the chin between the bottom of the lip and the bottom of the chin. Get someone to check this out for you from the side.

Step 5

FOCUS ON: The tongue

Focus on the feeling of the very tip of the tongue as it bounces off the reed to start the notes.

Use the mouthpiece and barrel for this step.

All notes are 'tongued' at the beginning of playing. The process of 'tonguing' is used to start the notes. Just as the very tip of the tongue is used to articulate the words we speak; the tip of the tongue is used to articulate the notes we play.

The tongue:

- Strikes the reed just underneath its tip.
- Activates the reed to vibrate then the vibrating air goes down the clarinet to produce the sound.

Spend lots of time learning to tongue. Follow the instructions precisely and do not move on until you are comfortable that you are tonguing well. This step is paramount.

Teachers usually have a preferred imaginary pronunciation of sound that they use when teaching their students to tongue. Some use the pronunciation of 'ta, ta, ta, ta,' others 'tee, tee, tee, tee,' and others 'doo, doo, doo, doo' or 'too, too, too, too'.

I will use the sound 'ta' in the instructions of how to tongue, but please feel free to imagine the pronunciations of the alternative sounds above if you wish.

Sense the movement of the tongue:

- Say 'ta, ta, ta, ta,' slowly, and put your mind on the movement of the tip of the tongue and sense its movements. Say it repeatedly. This is the movement the tongue uses to articulate the notes.

- Notice that:
  1. You use only the very tip of the tongue.
  2. The movement is from the front, not the back of the tongue.
  3. It moves only a short distance.
  4. It 'bounces' lightly and gently to make these sounds.

- Ask yourself where the tip of your tongue touches as you say 'ta, ta, ta, ta'.

  I hope your answer is that your tongue touches the gum just behind your top teeth. Try it again and see.

- Say one long 'Taaaaaaaaaaa' sound. Hold this on, imagining the air going through to the bottom of the clarinet.

Tongue one long note

Form your embouchure around the mouthpiece:

- Lower lip over the lower teeth, stretched to the sides.
- Reed resting on the bottom lip. Top teeth on top of the mouthpiece.
- 'Smile' at the mouth corners.

- Breathe in.
- Put the very tip of the tongue just underneath the tip of the reed (imagining that the tip of the reed is the gum just above your top teeth).
- As you push the air through the mouthpiece, bounce the tongue off the reed as if you are saying 'Taaaaaaaaa' – hold the sound on to play one very long note. You have activated the reed to vibrate and produced the sound.
- Practise playing this again, breathing in first, then pushing the column of air through the mouthpiece immediately as the tongue strikes the reed.

Tongue lots of notes

To make a series of notes, push the same long column of air through the mouthpiece and tongue the reed repeatedly as if pronouncing 'taa, taa, taa, taa'.

Understand these vital points from the onset!

- The aim is to use a single long note/column of air, and chop it up into a series of shorter notes by articulating the reed with the tongue.
- The aim is NOT to push single puffs of air into the clarinet to make each note. You should hear no gaps between a series of tongued notes.

Step 6

FOCUS ON: A flowing clarinet sound

Focus on how it feels to tongue the reed and push the air through the clarinet to produce the sound.

Use the whole assembled body of the instrument. Support the clarinet with your right thumb placed underneath the thumb rest. Put your left thumb on the thumb hole at the back of the clarinet and cover the first finger hole to finger the note ‘E’.

If you have thoroughly followed the previous steps in this exercise, this next part will seem a simple progression, and you will have launched sound production successfully. Here are the instructions which can be used for your revision in the future.

Form the embouchure:

- Make a cushion for the reed by turning a little of the lower lip over the teeth.
- Rest the reed in the centre as you stretch the lip to the sides.
- Put the top teeth down firmly on to the top of the mouthpiece.
- Breathe in through the sides of the mouth.
- Tongue the reed as you push an even air column through the clarinet. Imagine the air traveling through to the bottom of the instrument.

Engage with the feeling of:

- The slight 'smile' at the mouth corners as the muscle stretches sideways.
- The relaxed mouth as it breathes in and out naturally and how it never bites the mouthpiece.
- The simultaneous movement of the tongue striking the reed and the air flowing through the gap between the reed and the mouthpiece.

Well done!

Extra Embouchure Explanation – Are You Smiling?

It's important NOT to:

- Grip or bite the mouthpiece. This would close the gap between the reed and the mouthpiece tip, make the sound tight, and restrict or stop the sound.
- Puff the cheeks out. This makes the playing uncontrolled and the sound unfocused.

A smile is always the answer!

A good method of preventing embouchure problems is to always keep a slight 'smile' at the mouth corners. This is not a wide pronounced smile, just a small one where you stretch them out a little as if you were grinning. You are not really smiling of course, but stretching the mouth corners back slightly.

This helpful little stretch:

- Prevents the lips or the mouthpiece being pushed out as you push the air through the mouthpiece.
- Keeps the cheeks in so you will make a better sound and not look like a frog.
- Helps keep the chin nice and 'flat' preventing it from bunching upwards and closing the gap between the reed and the mouthpiece.

Strong embouchure muscles develop over time! Keep smiling!

The Best Tone Exercise

Want to make The Best Sound in Town? The easiest way is to play plenty of long notes – every day!

Now before you fall over in disappointment at what you may feel sounds like the most tedious exercise out, let me promise you that the playing of long notes is THE exercise that will lead to the best tone.

Long notes are simply a 'forever' exercise – one for today and every single time you play, one that will get your playing ship-shape in no time. As a beginner, you have enough information for now. You have just learned how to produce your sound – now you need to practise becoming familiar with the feeling of the mouthpiece in the mouth, what it feels like as you push the air through the mouthpiece and instrument, and dealing with supporting the clarinet in general. Long notes will develop these things for you.

Feel enthusiastic about playing long notes as they will give you the biggest benefits in the shortest amount of time. Play them at the beginning of every single practice session (perhaps ten long notes to start with), as a good warm up before you play your tunes and other exercises – even professional players do this!

Remember:

- **Long notes strengthen the embouchure**, in particular the muscles around the mouth which enclose the mouthpiece, enabling the player to play for more extended periods, control the sound and phrasing, and avoid biting the mouthpiece.
- **Long notes exercise the ears and listening skills**, as the player must continually focus on the quality of the tone to ensure the best result.
- **Long notes strengthen the diaphragm muscle** underneath the lungs, which controls the air as it's pushed out of the lungs and through the clarinet.

So how long is a long note?

Just play your long notes for as long as it feels comfortable and the sound is good. You will be surprised at the length that you can achieve once you get practising. Often at the end of the note, when you think that you are running out of breath, you can carry the note on for longer. The skill is to engage your diaphragm muscle underneath the lungs even more at the end of the note. You can revise the exercise 'Diaphragm Discovery' in Chapter 2 to practise this if you wish.

A word of caution here!

Never extend a long note if it creates a feeling of unpleasant physical discomfort. Controlling the breathing is a strange experience at first, and sometimes – but rarely – when a beginner overblows it can create a sense of light-headedness or even a fainting feeling. When a player gets used to the 'in and out' movements of the air, these feelings subside. Be mindful at the beginning of learning.

The key word is 'LISTEN'.

Your aim at the beginning is simply to make the best sound you can. Of course, you must **develop the habit of attentive listening.** Listen as hard as you can, as focused as you can, for all the time you are playing. With focused listening, you will get as much development and improvement from your practice time as possible.

Ask yourself **Sensible Sound Questions** when you are playing your long note exercises:

- Is my sound smooth and even or is it wobbling around?
- Is my note going sharp or flat? Is it going up in pitch or down in pitch?
- Is my tone sweet or harsh? Is it the best sound I can make?
- Is my sound 'tight' or 'open'? If your sound is tight, as if you were saying the sound 'eeeeee', tightening your throat, imagine making the sound of 'ahhhhh' which produces a much more 'open' tone.

If you listen hard, you will know the answers. You will be amazed how careful listening will lead to modifying the way you push the air through the clarinet to achieve a higher quality sound.

A Sound Summary

- Keep the tone 'even' – that means pushing the air through the clarinet evenly. In the beginning stages don't be tempted to create a vibrato – that's where the sound is slightly coloured and waivered and is a skill for later. Aim for smooth air control for now.

- Keep a 'flat chin' which is not bunched up to the reed. Check out the side view of the chin, and if the chin is going upwards, think 'jaw to floor' as you bring the jaw lower.

- Make sure you are not biting the mouthpiece.

- Relax the sides of the mouth to breathe in and tongue the beginning of the note.

- Control the air. Don't overblow or force the air or the sound will distort, the pitch will vary, or you might squeak.

- Imagine that your sound is carrying a long way and that the people in the next street can hear you. Have the idea that your sound is not just around the mouthpiece, but that it is projecting a long way beyond the room.

- Be patient, mature sounds evolve over time. Keep these words in mind – 'full', 'vibrant', 'open', 'even' and your sound will be heading in the right direction!

Keep practising!

There is an ULTIMATE BENEFIT for you – your sound quality will become pure, sweet, even, controlled, warm, gorgeous, appealing, and all the wholesome things that make people want to listen to it!

It's simply – The Best Sound in Town.

CHAPTER 4

Clarinet Note Fingerings

- Tips and Tricks for Easy Learning
- The First Notes, using the fingers of the left hand – 'E', 'D', 'C', 'F', 'F#', 'G', 'A' & throat 'Bb'
- The Next Notes, using the fingers of both hands – low 'B', 'Bb', 'A', 'G', 'F' & 'E'
- Approaching the Register Key and Clarion Register

Tips and Tricks for Easy Learning

Use this chapter:

- To learn the fingering for a new note and how to play it easily.
- To find the solution if there is a problem producing a note with clarity.

Here you will learn the usual notes studied by most beginners in the first weeks of lessons. These are the notes in the Chalumeau and Throat Registers of the instrument – the natural notes from low 'E' below the stave, to the 'A' in the second space up of the stave, plus 'F#' in the first space up, low 'Bb' and the 'Bb' on the middle line. At the end, you will find advice on how to approach the learning of the notes in the upper (Clarion) register and how to use the speaker key (sometimes called the register key) efficiently.

Each of the following pages is dedicated to the learning of one note in turn. Its position on the stave is clearly displayed and the fingerings are represented in these various ways:

- An image of the hands on the clarinet, fingering the note.
- A chart of 6 circles – representing the six main holes on the front of the clarinet. The three circles at the top represent those holes on the upper middle joint which are covered by the first three fingers of the left hand. The three circles at the bottom represent those on the lower middle joint played by the fingers of the right hand. If the hole is covered to produce the note, the circle is black. If it is left open, the circle is white.
- A numerical indication of the fingers is used – the first finger of the hand being '1', the second '2', third '3' and the little finger '4'.

There are certain guidelines to the playing and learning of all the notes. There may be too many to implement and remember all at once, but here they are for your support and reference. You can go back to these points at any time if you have challenges producing a note.

Remember

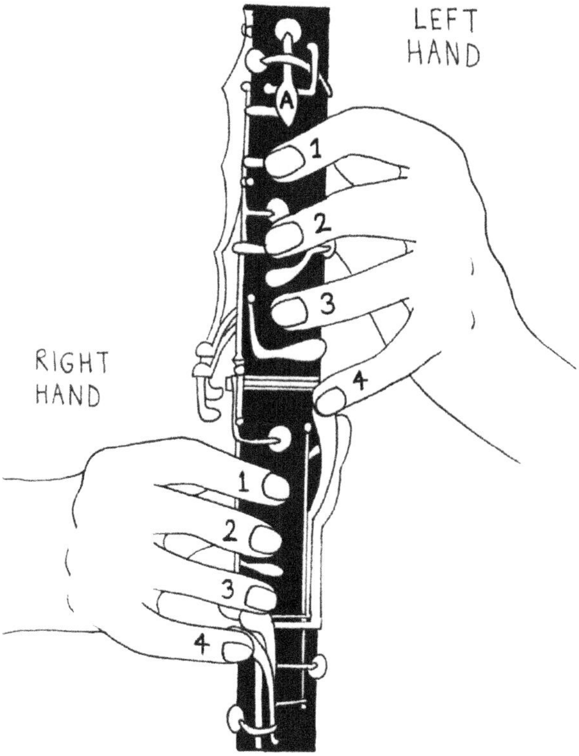

- Have both hands relaxed, keeping the natural 'C' shapes created by the first fingers and thumbs and **put the fingers on the holes so the middle fingers are at near right angles to the body of the clarinet.** You will then avoid touching the side keys near the first fingers which are responsible for unwelcomed squeaks when pressed by accident.
- **Arch the fingers** gently over the clarinet to activate each small knuckle to give strength and flexibility to the movements.
- **Keep all the fingers around the clarinet body** whether they are sealing the holes or not. Don't wave them high in the air a long way from the keys as this will slow down your technique.
- **Use the fleshy pads at the ends of the fingers to seal the holes**. Avoid putting the fingers too far over the holes.
- **Press the fingers firmly but without tension** on both the holes and the keys and make sure you press the ring keys that go around some of the holes.

The stability of the instrument

In the initial stages, the stability of the clarinet can be challenging when there are few fingers on the instrument. The clarinet might feel a bit wobbly at first.

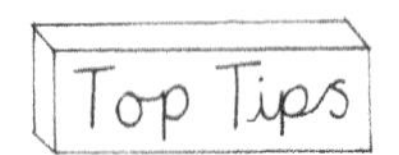

- **Nurture good support** in the correct way. Don't hold the instrument with your fist at the bottom. **Keep the lower thumb straight underneath the thumb rest and pull it upwards** a little. **Make good use of the sling** if you are using one and **give as much of the weight of the clarinet to the neckpiece as is possible.**

- **Don't try to hold the clarinet steady by gripping the mouthpiece between your lips**. Your mouth must be relaxed to make the best sound.

- **Never attempt to 'hold' the clarinet with your fingers** – it is their sole job to play the instrument!

- **Guide the clarinet away from you**, about 40° from the body and allow the air to flow through the instrument. Be especially mindful of this if using a sling.

- Learn to **'feel' your way around the clarinet instead of looking down to find the keys**. Looking down with the clarinet in your mouth will change the pitch of the note and may spoil your sound.

- **Persevere with any initial instability** you may experience as you will soon become familiar with handling the instrument – even if you are a very young beginner!

Playing the new notes

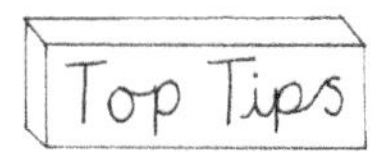

- Make sure you **have a good mouth position** (revise the exercise 'Six Steps to Easy Embouchure and Sound' in Chapter 3) and remember to **tongue the reed every time you play a new note.**
- Push an **even column of air** through the clarinet to **make an even sound**.
- **When having a challenge playing a low note**, consider that the air must travel a long way down the tube to get the note. Remember these 4 things – **press the fingers firmly, tongue the reed firmly, push the air firmly** and always checkout that **all the fingers seal the holes completely. If you can't get a low note, play down to it from one you can.**

Recognising the names of the notes quickly

- The names of the **notes in the spaces** of the stave **spell 'FACE'** going from the lower space upwards.
- The names of the **notes on the lines** are the initial letters of the line '**E**very **G**ood **B**oy **D**eserves **F**ootball'. Keep this in mind as you learn the notes in this chapter.

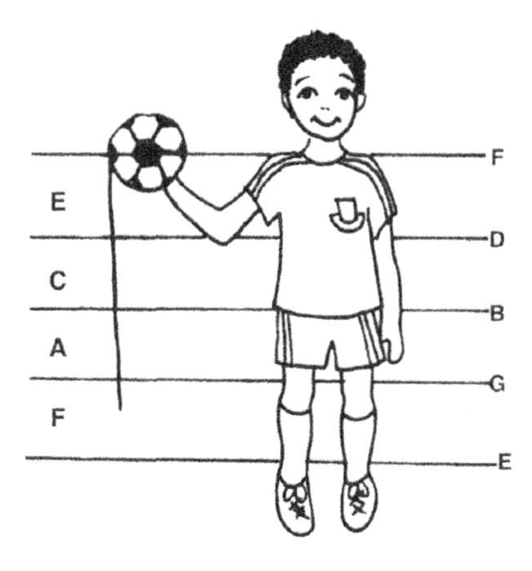

Above all…

Instead of merely absorbing facts, **make your learning a sensory experience from the start**. As you learn a new note, rather than just thinking and learning how many fingers it takes and on which holes to put them, create a wider experience.

Draw together and **associate your senses**:

- **LOOK at the position of the note on the stave**
- **LISTEN to the quality of the sound of the note**
- **FEEL the position of the fingerings on the instrument and the position of the mouth as you achieve the note**

You will both develop your aural ability and be surprised how quickly you read a note then instantly reproduce it on your instrument in the future.

NOTE 'E'

Written **ON the bottom line** of the stave.

Played with the **first finger and thumb** of the **left hand**.

NOTE 'D'

Written **directly underneath the stave.**

Played with the first **two fingers and thumb** of the **left hand.**

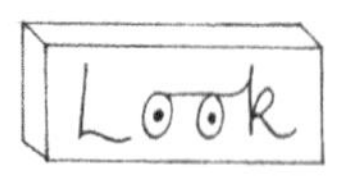

Notice that 'D' is in a space even though it is underneath the stave – it doesn't have a line through it.

NOTE 'C'

Written **ON the first ledger line below the stave.**

Played with the **first three fingers and the thumb** of the **left hand.**

Remember

Keep the middle finger at a right angle to the clarinet as this will help you to avoid touching the side key underneath the first finger.

NOTE 'F'

Written **IN the bottom space** of the stave.

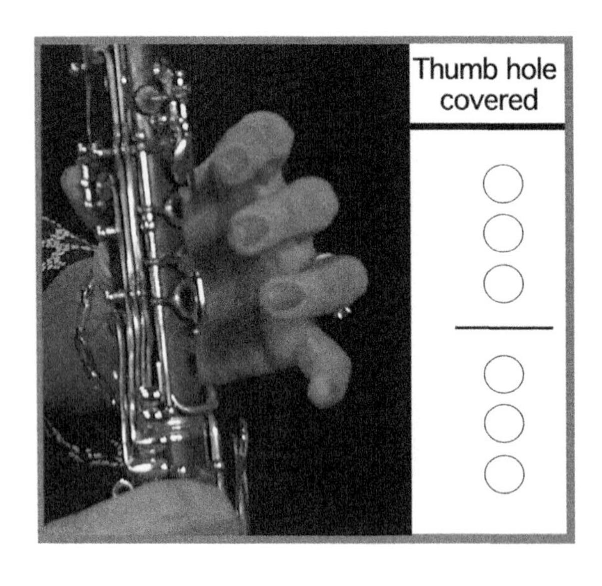

Played with **the thumb** only of the **left hand.**

Do this please

Pull upwards with the lower thumb to help stabilise the instrument.

NOTE 'F#'

Written **IN the bottom space** of the stave.

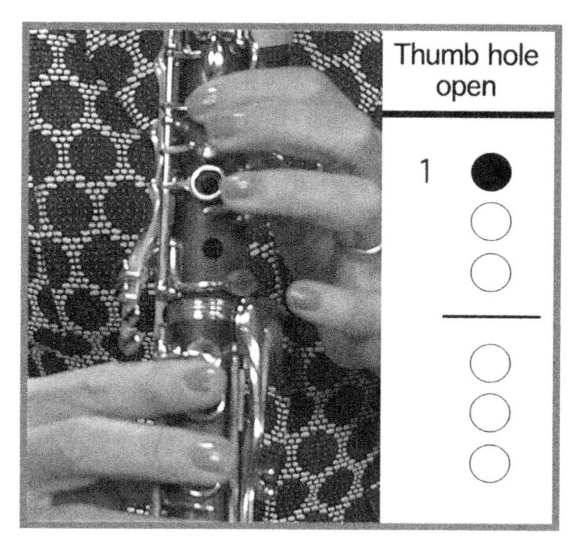

Played with the **first finger** of the **left hand.**

Remember

Keep the thumb clear of the thumb hole when playing 'F#' but do not put it on the body of the clarinet. Keep it a small distance behind the hole.
A sharpened note raises a natural note by a semitone.
The sharp sign # is written before the note on the stave.

NOTE 'G'

Written **ON the second line** of the stave.

Played with **no fingers or thumb**.

Look

This note is often called 'open G' as all the holes are left open to play it. It's also referred to as 'throat G' as it's created in the throat area of the clarinet.

NOTE 'A'

Written **IN the second space** up of the stave.

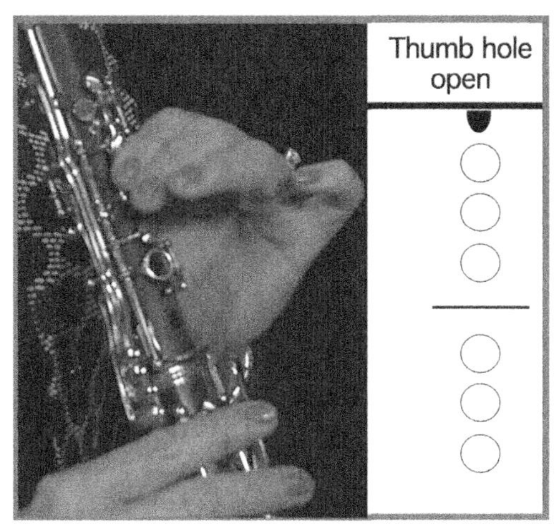

Played by **pressing the tip of the 'A' key** with the **side of the first finger** of the **left hand**. All the other holes are open.

Play this:

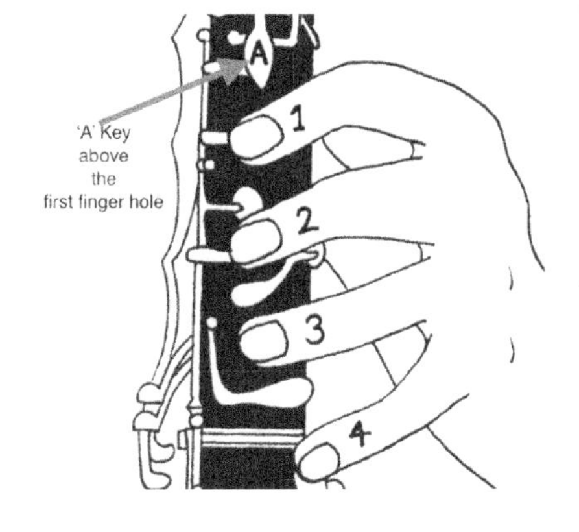

Twist your wrist very slightly to press the tip of the 'A' key with the side of the finger. It is not necessary to lift the finger high up on to the key. Practise a gentle rolling motion by playing 'A', 'G', 'A', 'G' / on, off, on, off repeatedly until the movement is fluent. Keep the other fingers around the clarinet and don't wave them a long way from the keys with the twisting action.

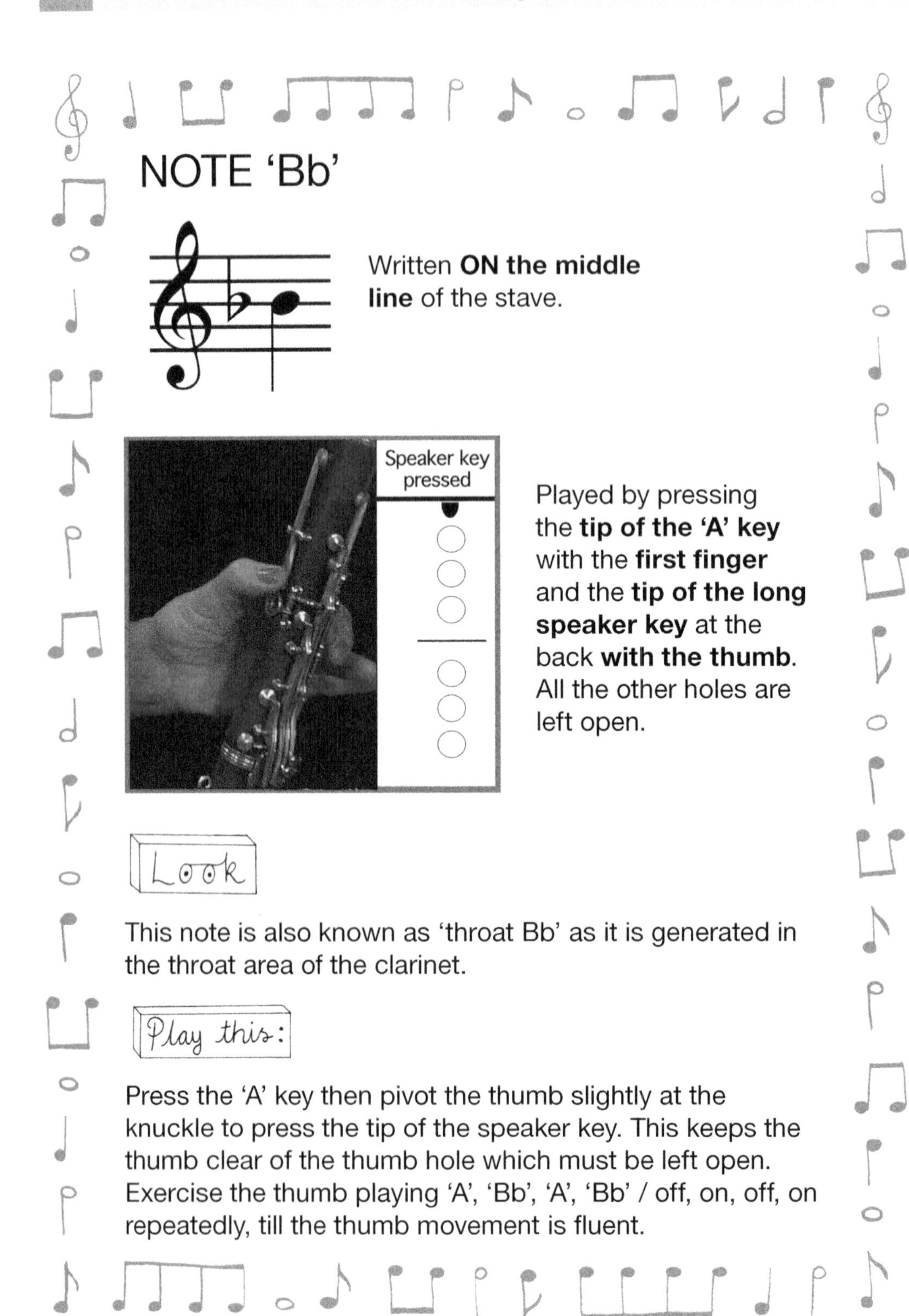

NOTE 'Bb'

Written **ON the middle line** of the stave.

Played by pressing the **tip of the 'A' key** with the **first finger** and the **tip of the long speaker key** at the back **with the thumb**. All the other holes are left open.

Look

This note is also known as 'throat Bb' as it is generated in the throat area of the clarinet.

Play this:

Press the 'A' key then pivot the thumb slightly at the knuckle to press the tip of the speaker key. This keeps the thumb clear of the thumb hole which must be left open. Exercise the thumb playing 'A', 'Bb', 'A', 'Bb' / off, on, off, on repeatedly, till the thumb movement is fluent.

NOTE 'LOW B'

Written **underneath the first ledger line below the stave.**

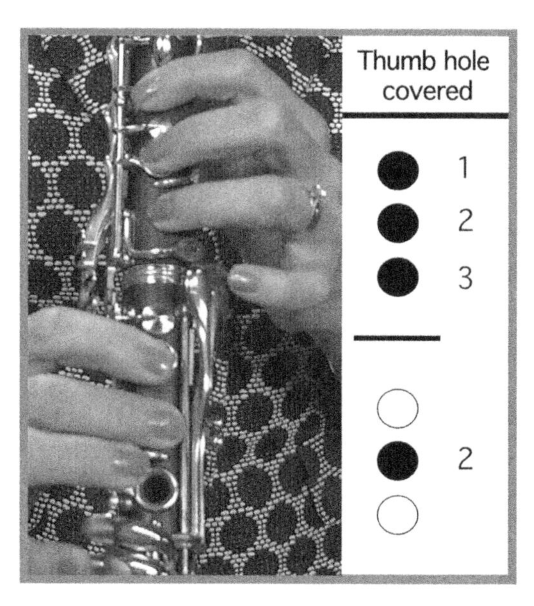

Played with the **first three fingers and thumb of the left hand** and the **second finger of the right hand.**

NOTE 'LOW Bb'

Written **underneath the first ledger line below the stave.**

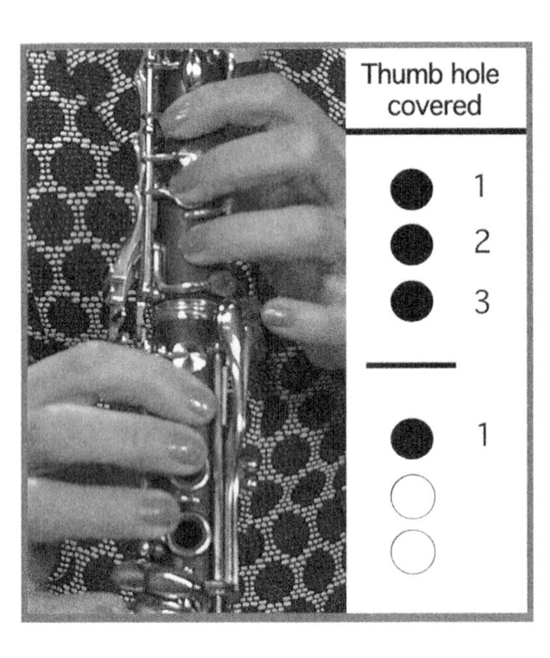

Played with the **first three fingers and thumb of the left hand** and the **first finger of the right hand.**

NOTE 'LOW A'

Written **ON the second ledger line below the stave.**

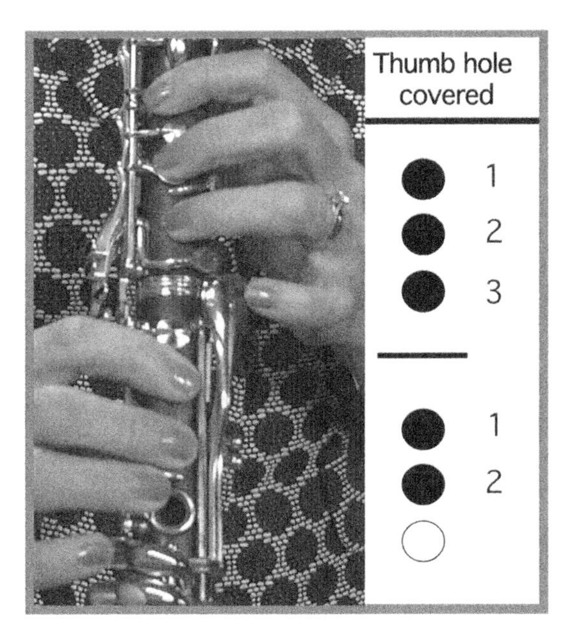

Played with the **first three fingers and thumb of the left hand** and the **first two fingers of the right hand.**

Top Tips

FEEL the holes underneath your fingers and SENSE them completely covering the holes and pressing the ring keys down too.

NOTE 'LOW G'

Written **underneath the second ledger line** below the stave.

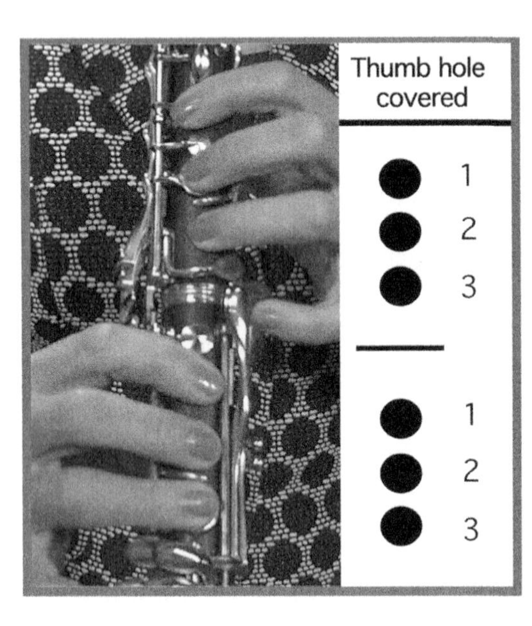

Played with the **first three fingers and the thumb of the left hand** and the **first three fingers of the right hand.**

Top Tips

To play a low note you don't know, play down to it from a higher note that you can play easily.
Play 'C', 'B' 'A' 'G' Push the air through the instrument firmly and hold the 'G' on to make a substantial note.

NOTE 'LOW F'

Written **ON the third ledger line** below the stave.

Played with the **first three fingers and thumb of the left hand**, the **first three fingers of the right hand** and the **'F' key pressed by the little finger of the right hand.**

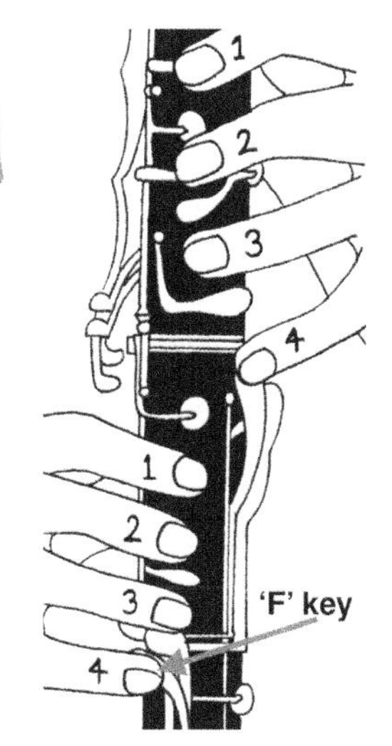

Remember

The Low Note Rules:

- **Firm Fingers**
- **Firm Air Column**
- **Firm Tongue**

Play this:

- Play 'C', 'B', 'A' and hold the 'A' for as long as you can.
- Play 'B', 'A', 'G' and hold the 'G' for as long as you can.
- Play 'A', 'G', 'F' and hold the 'F' for as long as you can.

Appreciate and memorise the feeling of the mouth and fingers as you play the long 'F' note so you will be able to get it easily in the future.

NOTE 'LOW E'

Written **below the third ledger line** below the stave.

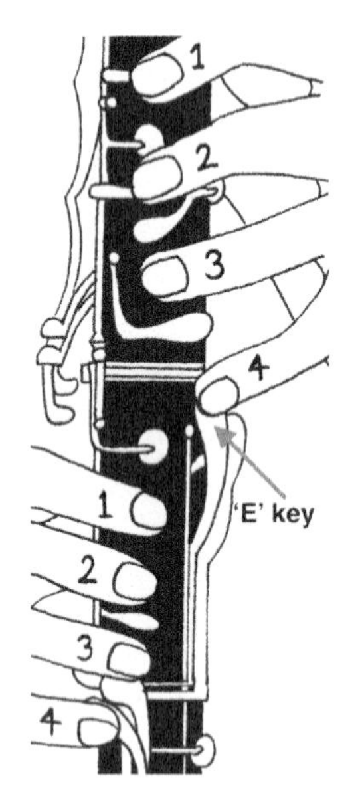

Played with the **first three fingers and the thumb of the left hand,** the **first three fingers of the right hand** and the **fourth finger of the left hand on the 'E' key** which is the longest key on the left. It is helpful to also **press the 'F' key with the right hand fourth finger** in the beginning stages of learning, as this will support you getting the 'E' with more certainty.

Play this:

- 'C', 'B', 'A', 'G' Tongue the 'C' then put the rest of the fingers down and hold the 'G' for as long as you can.

  Play the next notes in the same way.

- 'B', 'A', 'G', 'F' press the right 'F' key firmly.
- 'A', 'G', 'F', 'E' press both the little fingers firmly. Remember the position of the mouth as you play 'E'.

Approaching the Register Key and Clarion Register

The range of notes from the 'B' on the middle line of the stave to the 'C' above the stave is called the 'Clarion register' which you will learn after becoming familiar with the lower notes. Here are some tips for when you learn them.

- The register key at the back of the clarinet is also known as the 'speaker key'. It is pressed open for all the notes in the high Clarion register.
- The *tip* of the speaker key is pressed with the *tip* of the left hand thumb *whilst the thumb covers the thumb hole.*
- By pressing the speaker key the clarinet plays the note which is a twelfth higher than the note without the speaker key.

Going from the low notes, that don't use the speaker key, to the high notes that do, and vice versa, is called **'crossing the break'.**

Tips for 'crossing the break'

- Keep the column of air strong when you cross the break. Push out firmly at the waist as you push the air through to the high notes.
- Do not stop the air, between the notes when crossing the break.
- Make sure that your reed is not too soft to play the high notes. When starting to learn these you may have to go up a strength of reed.
- Make sure the top teeth are firmly on the top of the mouthpiece and that the clarinet is not wobbling in your mouth. Don't bite, think 'jaw to floor' to keep the gap between the reed and the mouthpiece open.
- Check all the fingers are covering the necessary holes. You will need to give the thumb hole special attention at the beginning.

PART TWO

Read, Count, Play, Enjoy!

- You CAN Read Music!
- Got your Finger on the Pulse? – Be Pulse Aware!

You CAN Read Music!

Reading music is EASY! I promise you. Just as we can learn to be literate and read and understand books, we can learn to read and interpret music. Sometimes people view the written parts as a complex, indecipherable foreign language or code that won't crack. They shy away from trying to understand, adding it to their, often false, set of reasoning why 'I'm not musical'. This section breaks down any mystery.

There is an approach to reading that is straightforward and easy to understand. The steps are introduced gradually and will make sense as you learn to apply a 'method' to interpret the written parts for yourself.

In 'Read, Count, Play, Enjoy', the concepts and notes are introduced sequentially, at a level which is the most comfortable for a beginner's understanding and technical ease.

This section of the book is a 'doing section' as well as reading. There are rhythm exercises to count, and tunes and exercises to play. All of these will reinforce your learning. Bringing together the reading aspects and playing skills, you are guided to support the air through the phrases. You will learn where to breathe so that the music makes sense and feels good to play.

Embracing the requirements for the first lessons, the next three chapters will introduce you to:

- The awareness and importance of the pulse.
- The first music signs and symbols.
- How to feel and count the first rhythms.
- How to play the first tunes and exercises.

For the next lessons the later chapters teach:

- The next signs and symbols.
- How to count quaver/eighth rhythms and dotted notes.
- The concepts of key and scales.

- How to slur.
- The 'Three Step System for Reading Music'.
- How to play the next lessons exercises, scales and tunes.
- How to address and sort out a problem.
- How to practise.

Learn this material in sequence to gradually increase your understanding and strengthen your skill sets.

Got your Finger on the Pulse? – Be Pulse Aware!

When we think about reading music, we think about looking at and interpreting the written notes – yet there is a vital core factor that can't be seen because it can't be written down!

Of course, it is the PULSE. **When we play with a feeling and an awareness of the pulse, our playing becomes ALIVE.** We feel the pulse and think the counting to it. We don't THINK a pulse – we FEEL it. We engage with energy inside us, the inner aliveness, and wilfully sense a pulse to play to. I am sure you will have heard players whose music seems lifeless and flat while others' performances sound vibrant and attractive.

As the pulse is THE most important factor about music of any kind, it necessitates primary attention in this section, before we deal with all the signs and symbols of the written stuff.

Consider this – do you like pop music? If so, what's your favourite tune? Think carefully. Why exactly do you like that tune? What is the element about it that engages you and compels you to listen? Think about the answer before you read on.

I'm sure that your answer will have something to with how you feel when you hear that tune. Does it affect your senses and stir your emotions in some way? Does it make you tap your foot or get up and dance? Maybe it simply makes you feel happy.

It has always been the case that modern-day pop music is accepted and appreciated worldwide by young people. With its pulse and vibrant feel, it's at the core of most young peoples' social engagement. The drummer is the indispensable backbone of most pop tunes. Even if people think they are engaging with the lyrics of a song, it's usually the pulse, laid down by the drummer, that draw them in, that they tap their foot to, and get up and dance to.

Be alert to the music in your everyday that appeals to you. Sense the pulse – if you're listening to pop music, the easiest way is to listen out for the drummer! Become 'Pulse Aware' from now on as it will help you in your playing.

As listeners, we engage with the pulse and energy of a tune.
As performers, it's our responsibility to engage our audience by delivering our playing with a sense of pulse and energy too.

Sometimes, people refer to 'playing with a pulse' and at other times 'playing with a beat'. Jazz players talk about sitting in 'the groove' of the beat. You can interpret these as meaning the same thing.

When a group of musicians perform together, they all play with the same pulse, keeping the music parts together. The conductor or leader will decide on, or 'set the pulse', and indicate this to the players before the music begins. The individual performers do not determine their own pulse – if they did, they would simply not play together!

When you play on your own, it is imperative that you sense and set your pulse before you play and continue to play to that pulse throughout.

How does a beginner start feeling and sensing a beat? Just go out for a walk, or simply stand up and walk on the spot. Observe the regularity of your even steps and count them as you go along – '1, 2, 3, 4, 1, 2, 3, 4'. Sense the movement of your body as you move and appreciate that there is a regular and even pulse within you as you walk.

NOTE – you are doing two things here – you are both *thinking* about the pulse, and more importantly, you are *feeling* the pulse as a sensory movement within yourself.

After a while, increase your speed and walk faster – you have increased the tempo. Notice how even and steady the fast speed is, and feel the pace within you. Again, count with the movement of your feet as you go along. Walk very slowly too – it feels different to walk slower. Appreciate and connect with the sensory movement of each step. Count again along with the movement of the feet and carefully place the counting exactly with the movement of each step – '1, 2, 3, 4, 1, 2, 3, 4' as you walk.

You CAN feel and sense a pulse.
From now on, you are 'Pulse Aware'!

CHAPTER 5

LEARN the First Signs and Symbols

- Notes Have Values
- The Stave
- Notes Have Names
- Bars and Bar Lines
- Repeat Sign and Time Signature

Here we go with all those exciting signs and symbols. Take this chapter one step at a time and read through all the charts to get an introductory overview. It's not necessary to memorise everything at once because all will fit into place as you go along. You will develop a gradual understanding of how to interpret what you see and turn the written notes into some live, vibrant music. Remember these are only the signs and symbols of the sounds that we are dealing with. The real music comes from inside you.

Notes Have Values

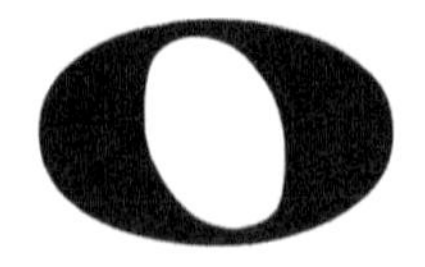

A white note without a stem is a semibreve. The American name is a whole note.

The semibreve/whole note has a value of 4 counts – '1, 2, 3, 4'
It is a – 've – ry – long – note'!

The semibreve/whole note rest looks like a box HANGING BELOW the fourth line up of the stave.

When you see this think 'shh, shh, shh, shh' as you count '1, 2, 3, 4'.

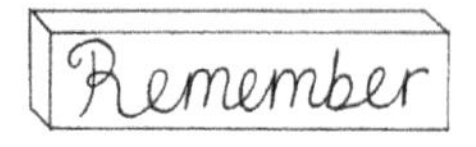

The 'stave' is the set of five lines on which the music is written.

A white note with a stem is a minim. The American name for the minim is a half note.

The minim/half note has a value of 2 counts.

A minim/half note rest looks like a box sitting ON the third line up of the stave.

As you count this rest '1, 2' also think 'shh, shh'.

Remember

Stems on notes can go either up or down.

A black note with a stem is a crotchet. The American name is a quarter note.

The crotchet/quarter note lasts for one beat or count.

Crotchet rest.

Don't play for 1 beat, have a rest 'shh'.

Remember

Sometimes a crotchet/quarter note rest looks a bit like a backwards number 7 – though it is usually shown as above.

The quaver is black note with a flag at the end of the stem. In America, this is an eighth note.

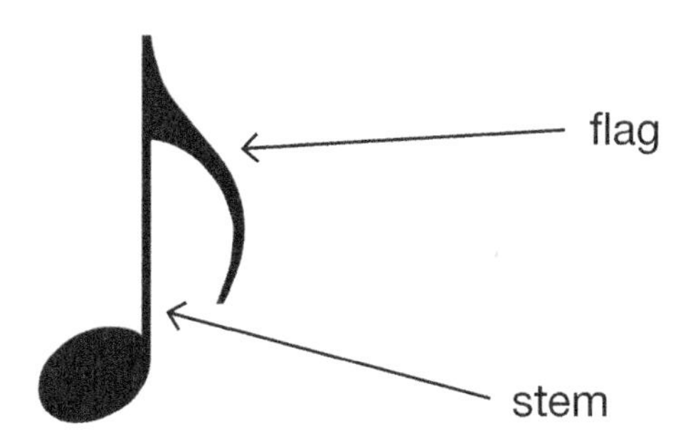

The quaver/eighth note has a length or value of half a beat. There are two quaver notes in the same space as a crotchet beat.

They are written in several ways.

Quavers together are grouped and joined by one line at the ends of their stems.

The quaver/eighth note rest look rather like a number 7.

Don't play for half a beat!

Table of Note Values

Note	English name	Value	American Name	Rest
𝅝	Semibreve	4 beats	Whole note	𝄻
𝅗𝅥	Minim	2 beats	Half note	𝄼
♩	Crotchet	1 beat	Quarter note	𝄽
♪	Quaver	1/2 beat	Eighth note	𝄾

The Stave

Music notes are written on five lines called the stave.
They are written both ON the lines and IN the
spaces between the lines.

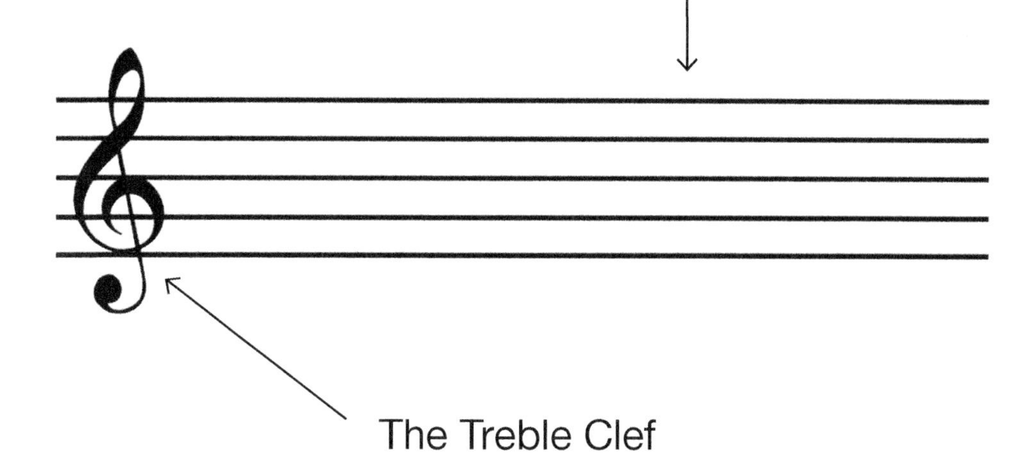

This sign positions the names and the pitches of the notes as they are written on the stave. The higher sounding the note the higher it is placed on the stave.

The clef curls around the second line up. That is the line on which the note ‘G’ is written.

Sometimes the treble clef is called the ‘G’ Clef.

Note IN a space

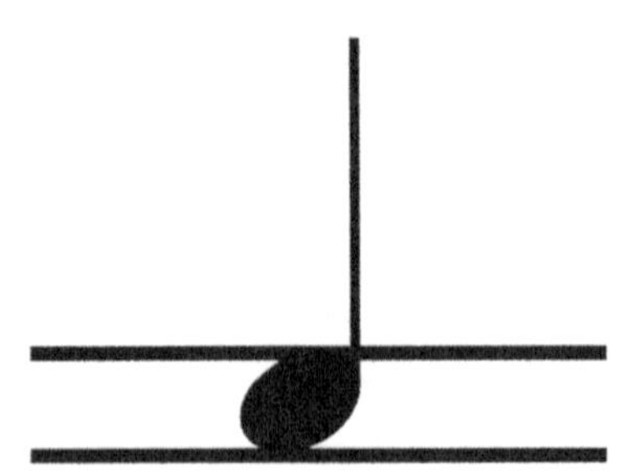

Note ON a line

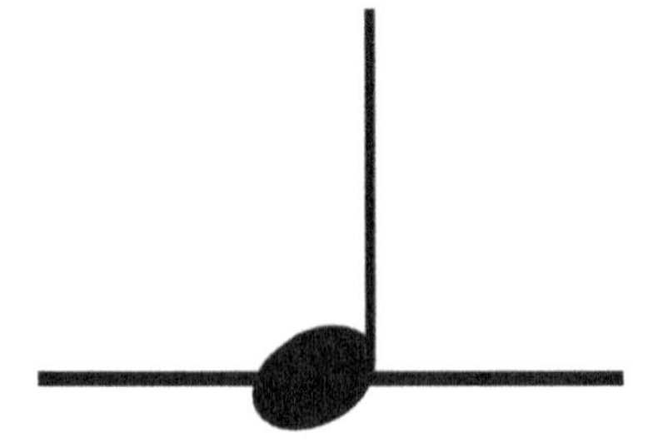

Ledger Lines

Above or below the stave the small lines are called 'Ledger Lines'

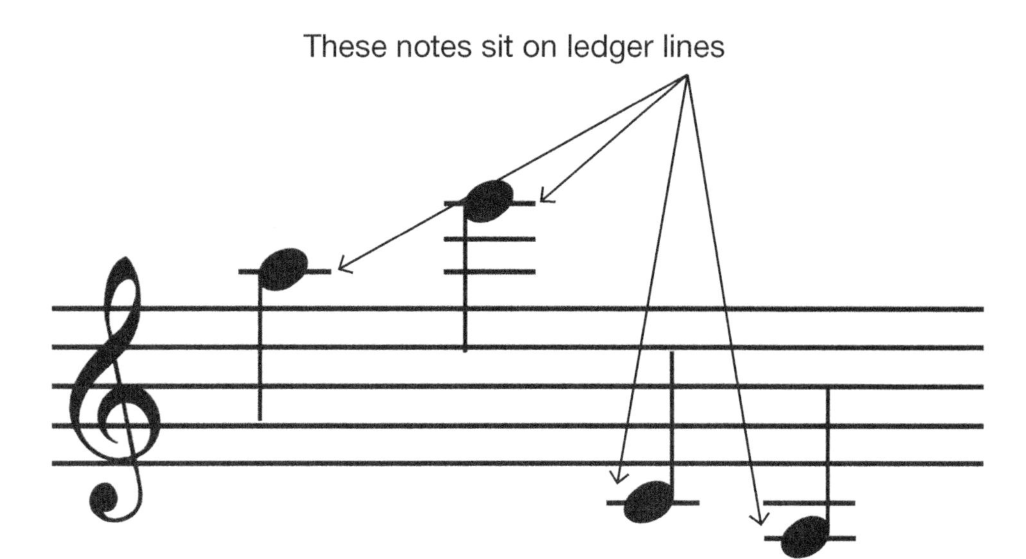

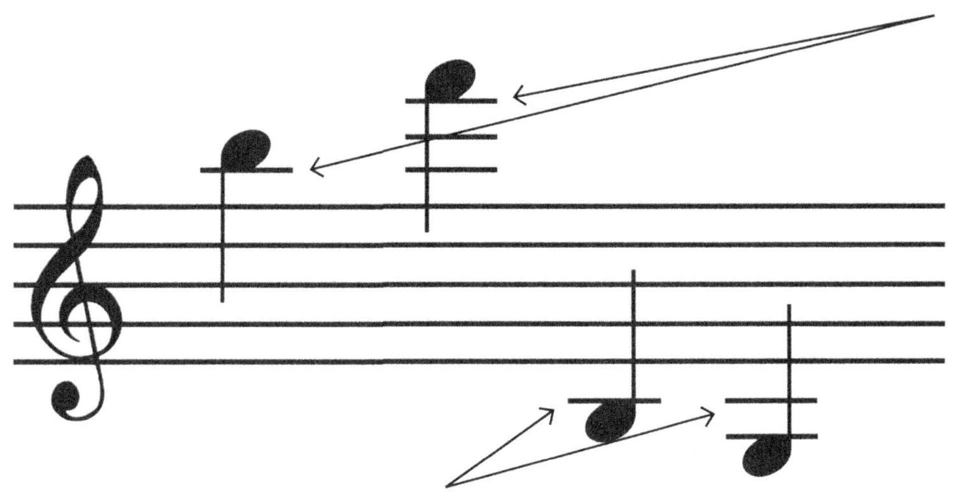

Notes Have Names

Music notes are simply named after the first seven letters of the alphabet.

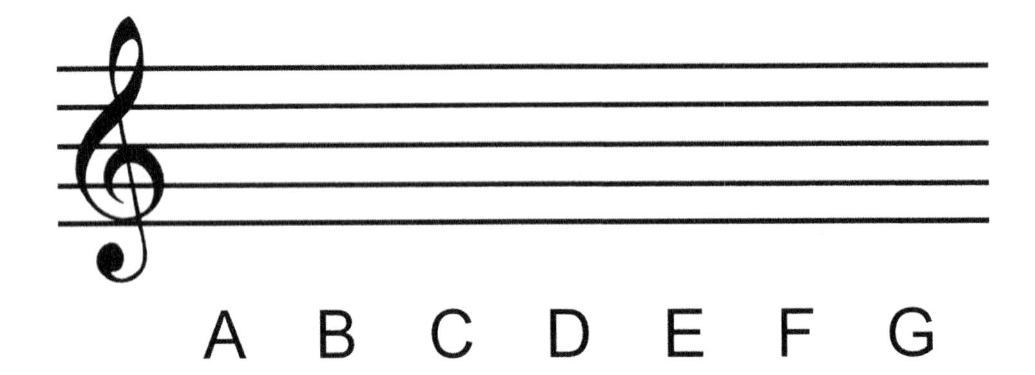

Names ON the Lines

There is a phrase which helps us to remember the names of the notes ON the lines.

'Every Good Boy Deserves Football'

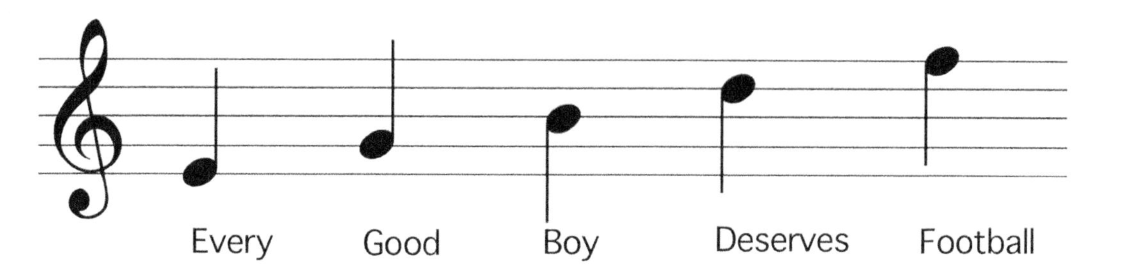

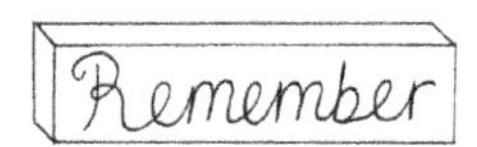

Starting from the bottom line, the initial letter of each word tells us the name of the note that is written on that line.

Memorise this phrase to assist you with quick note recognition.

Names IN the Spaces

Starting from the bottom, the names in the spaces spell FACE.

All the Note Names Together

Some notes are IN the spaces – some are ON the lines!

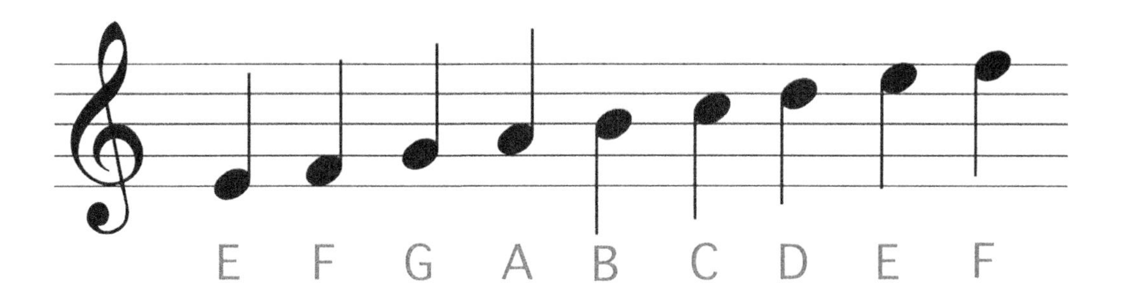

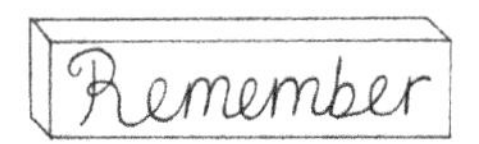

Notice that after the note 'G', the note names start again with 'A', then ascend alphabetically up the stave.

The lower pitched notes are written towards the bottom of the stave. As the notes ascend higher and higher in pitch they are written further up the stave.

Bars and Bar Lines

Music notes are written in small units called bars.

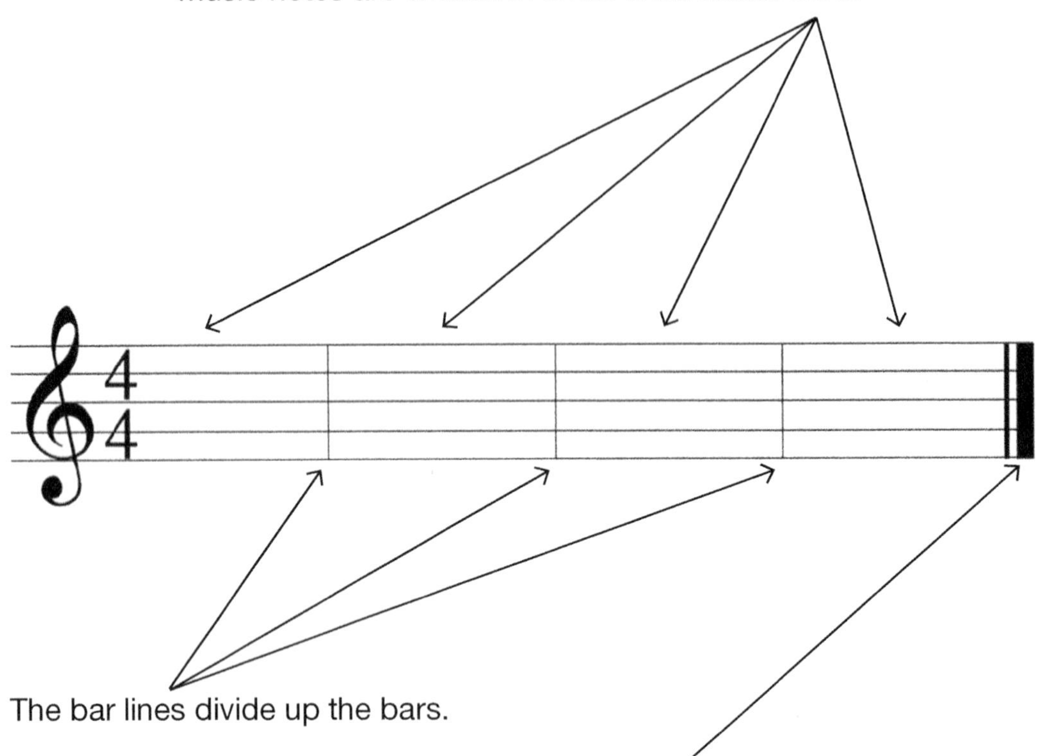

The double bar line at the end tells us that is the end of the piece.

Repeat Sign and Time Signature

There are dots in the spaces before the double bar line. This is a repeat sign meaning go back to the beginning and play the piece again.

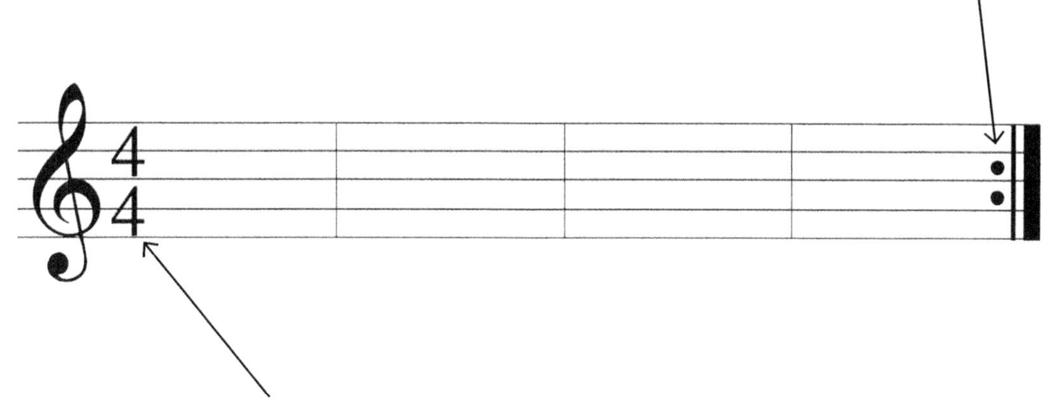

There are two numbers at the beginning of the piece, after the treble clef sign, one on top of the other. This is the time signature. The number at the top tells us the number of beats there are in each bar. The lower number shows us the value of the beat.

For example, a time signature of 4/4 means that there are four beats to the value of a crotchet/quarter note in each bar.

As a beginner, you do not have to pay much attention to understanding the lower number yet. Be aware of the meaning of the top number.

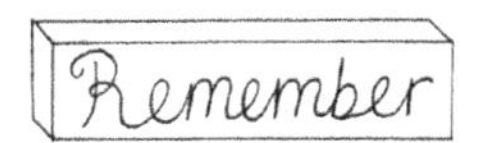

Most of the pieces you play at the beginning will have four beats in each bar. Instead of numbers indicating the time you may see a sign, like a letter 'C' meaning 'Common Time'. 4/4 and 'C' mean the same.

CHAPTER 6
COUNT the First Rhythms

- You Got Rhythm?
- Set the Pulse and 'Count Yourself In'
- Note and Rest Placements in the Bar. Let's Get Counting!
- Write the Counting & Mark Your Answers

You Got Rhythm?

We are already aware of the vital, life giving element of the pulse in music. The pulse is the base for yet another important aspect – that of RHYTHM.

The rhythm of the music is the movement of the different lengths of the notes over and on the pulse.

When learning to read music, the counting of the rhythm is a necessary skill from day one, and it's easy once you know how:

- With accurate counting, the right notes sit in the right place within the bar; then the music makes sense. Without counting, the music will not fit with the pulse. It will be all over the place, and no one will listen.
- Precise counting habits give you the confidence to read independently without the help of anyone else.

> **FACT**: If you cannot count the rhythm out loud, you will not be able to count and play at the same time either!

Do not skip this chapter! Follow every instruction through, step by step. Make counting an ingrained habit from the onset and learn to count the rhythms aloud before you play the tune. Give the rhythm reading your full attention without dealing with the technical handling of the clarinet at the same time. Once you have learned to count the rhythms you will then be able to play the music as you THINK the counting to the pulse you FEEL. Your music will flow with the pulse and you will draw in the listener as you play 'rhythmically'. After a period, you will find that rhythmical playing becomes habitual and you become less conscious of the constant counting in your head as you play. You will count automatically. The rhythm will flow with the underlying pulse and current of the music.

The following pages gradually introduce you to a method of counting the rhythm that you can use when learning to read any piece of music in the future. If you follow all the instructions and exercises precisely, as asked, you will find the method easy to apply when you play the tunes in the later chapters of this book.

Set the Pulse and 'Count Yourself In'

To count the rhythm of the notes in the bar, you must first set the pulse. You will then count the rhythm of the notes to that pulse.

RULE: Set the pulse **before** you start!

The setting of the pulse is often overlooked by many beginners in their haste to get playing, but spending time preparing the pulse is the most vital part of reading successfully. Starting without a prior sense of the speed, and playing with little pulse awareness, is an absolute waste of time as the music will be lifeless and lumpy.

It is sensible to work with a slow pulse, as this will give you plenty of time to think the counting as you go along.

The **'Count In'** is the counting that takes place **before** the music starts.

Once you have established your even, steady pulse you can then 'count yourself in'.

This ensures you experience a prior 'feel' and an awareness of the pulse. Just as a conductor indicates the speed of the pulse with the baton before the playing starts, a player can communicate the pulse to other musicians in the group by 'counting in' so they all play in unison. When playing alone it is vital that you 'count yourself in' so your playing will flow along with the pulse you sense inside.

If a piece has three beats in the bar, the 'count in' is '1, 2, 3'. If there are two beats in each bar, the 'count in' is '1, 2' and if there are four beats in the bar, it is '1, 2, 3, 4'.

Note and Rest Placements in the Bar. Let's Get Counting!

In the following exercises, the notes and rests are written on one line for simplicity.

There are four beats per bar in each exercise – hence the 'count in' is '1, 2, 3, 4'.

Note the places in the bar, in which the notes and rests sit. They are counted relative to their place within the bar. For example, a one-beat crotchet on the first beat of the bar would be counted as '1'. A two-beat minim, sitting on the first beat of the bar, would be counted as '1, 2' as it is played *through* the first *and* the second counts. A two-beat minim sitting on the third beat of the bar would be counted as '3, 4'.

When I ask you to count the exercises aloud please do this with lots of energy and enthusiasm and don't quietly count in your head. Counting aloud brings so much more vitality into what you are doing. You are sowing the seeds of bringing your music to life.

The following exercises focus on the placement of one note or rest value in turn. Count them all out loud with confidence and focus on keeping your counting sitting with the pulse. Read all the advice on each page as it will show you how to make sense of what you see so you will be able to understand independently, without guidance in the future.

Count crotchets, American name - quarter notes

A crotchet is recognised as a black note with a stem. It has a value of one count.

LOOK and THINK through what you see:

- There is a 4 beat 'count in' before the music starts.
- The top number of the time signature tells us there are four counts in a bar.
- The four one-beat notes have a different position within the bar.
- The first crotchet is in the first place in the bar – number '1'.
- The second crotchet is on the second count so it is counted as '2'.
- The third, on the third count, is number '3'.
- And in fourth place, the fourth crotchet is counted as number '4'.

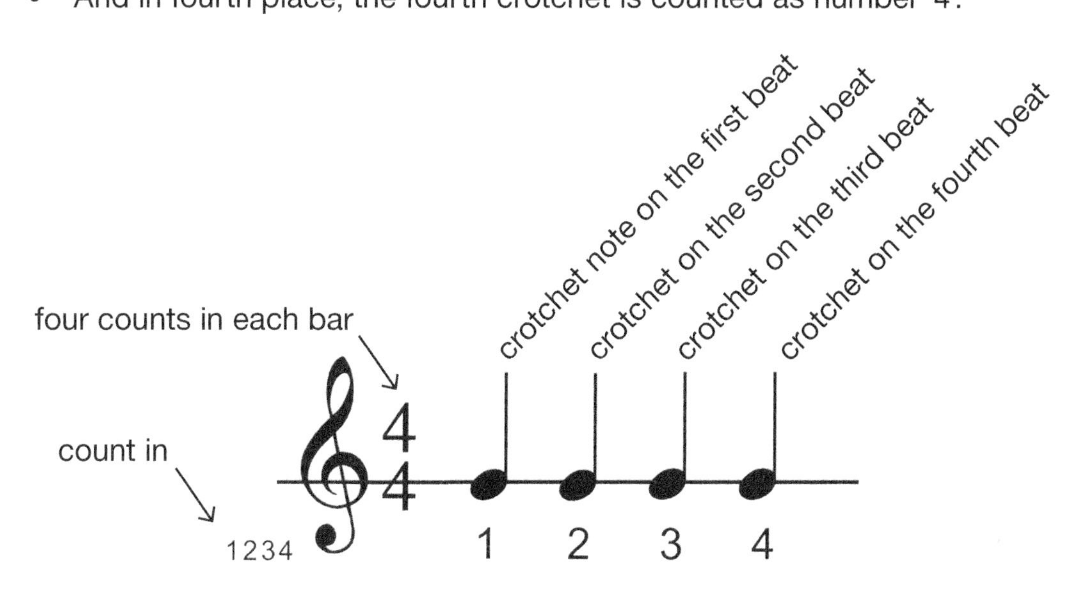

Follow these steps:

- FEEL and sense a slow pulse before you begin counting.
- COUNT aloud a bar's worth of beats, in '1, 2, 3, 4'.
- TAP each number of the 'count in' then the numbers underneath the notes with your finger as you continue to count aloud.
- LOOK and follow the notes as they go by.

Count minims, American name - half notes

The minim is recognised as a white note with a stem. It has a value of two counts.

LOOK and THINK through what you see:

- There is a 4 beat 'count in' before the music starts.
- There are four counts in a bar.
- There are two minim notes in this bar, each lasting through two counts.

  The first minim sits on the first beat of the bar and is played *through* the first and the second counts. It is counted as '1, 2'.

  The next minim sits on the third beat of the bar. It is played *through* the third and fourth beats and is counted as '3, 4'.

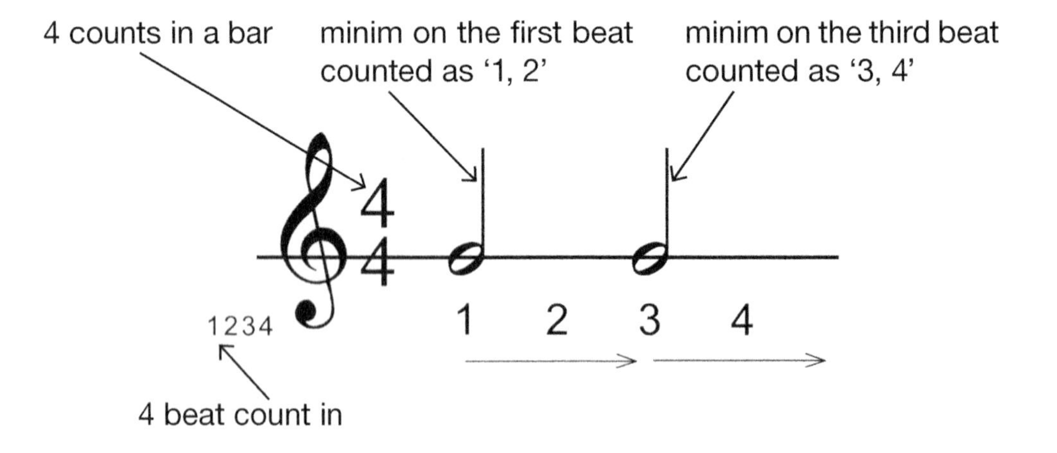

Follow these steps:

- FEEL and sense a slow pulse before you begin counting.
- COUNT aloud a bar's worth of beats, in '1, 2, 3, 4'.
- TAP each number of the 'count in' and the numbers underneath the notes with your finger.
- LOOK and follow the notes as they go by.

Count a semibreve, American name - whole note

A semibreve is a white note without a stem. It has a value of four counts.

LOOK and THINK. Take time to understand the symbols that are written down:

- There are two bars which are divided by a bar line.
- The number 4 at the top of the time signature indicates four counts in each bar.
- There are 4 one-beat crotchets in the first bar.
- In the second bar, there is a semibreve, counted as '1, 2, 3, 4'.

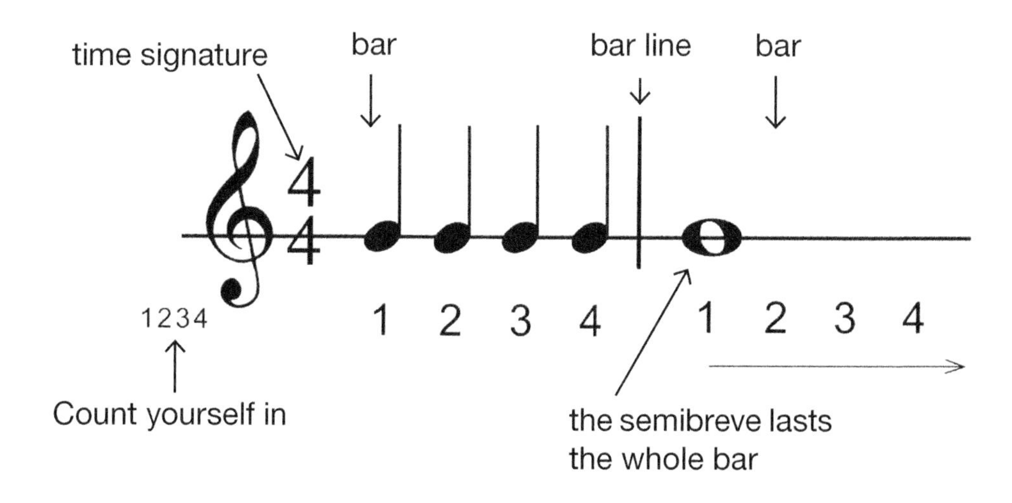

Follow these steps:

- FEEL and sense a slow pulse before you begin counting.
- COUNT aloud a bar's worth of beats, in '1, 2, 3, 4'.
- TAP each number of the 'count in' then the numbers underneath the notes with your finger as you count aloud.
- LOOK and follow the notes as they go by.

Count the crotchet / quarter note rest

The value of a crotchet rest is one count – 'shh'.

LOOK and THINK. Notice that in each bar:

- There are 4 beats.
- The crotchet notes sit on the first and second beats.
- The crotchet rests sit on the third and fourth beats.

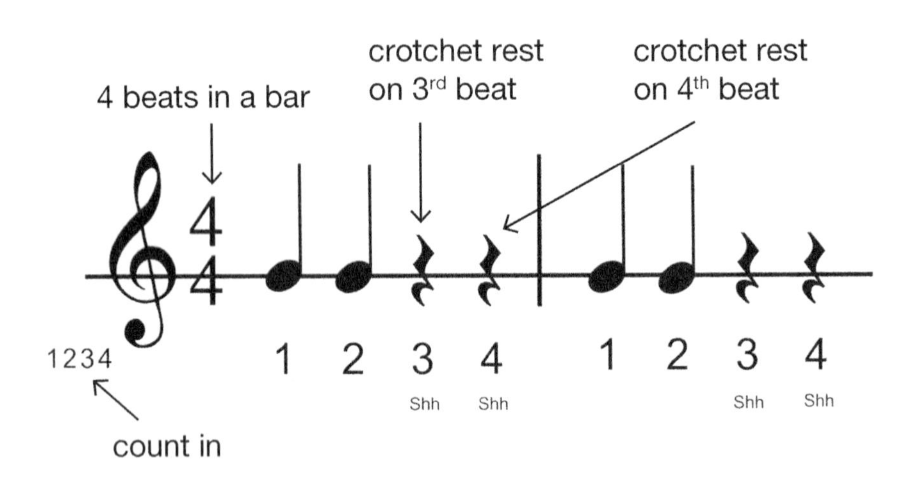

Follow these steps:

- FEEL and sense a slow pulse before you begin counting.
- COUNT in and TAP each number with your finger.
- LOOK and follow the notes and rests as they go by. Count the rests too.
- Either THINK 'shh' as you count each rest OR WHISPER the number as you count.

Count the minim / half note rest

The minim rest SITS ON a line. It has a value of two counts – 'shh, shh'.

LOOK and THINK:

- There is a four beat 'count in' indicated before the tune starts.
- The two-beat minim note sits on the first beat. It is counted as '1, 2'.
- The rest sits on the third beat and is counted as '3, 4'. It lasts *through* both the third and the fourth counts.

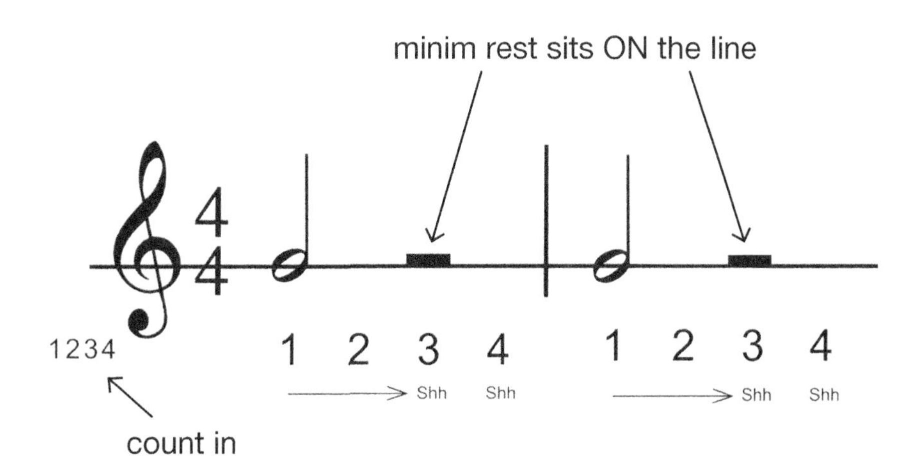

Follow these steps:

- FEEL and set the pulse.
- COUNT in, and TAP each number with your finger as you LOOK and follow the notes and rests as they go by.
- Either THINK 'shh, shh' as you count each rest OR WHISPER the number as you count.

Count the semibreve / whole note rest

This rest HANGS UNDERNEATH a line. It has a value of four beats. It lasts *through* four counts.

Notice the difference in appearance between the minim rest which SITS ON a line and the semibreve rests which HANG UNDERNEATH a line. The following might help you to remember which is which. Think 'M for Minim, M for Mountain'. Imagine a picture of a mountain solidly ON the ground. The minim rest SITS ON the line like a mountain SITS ON the ground. Think 'S for Semibreve, S for Submarine'. Picture a submarine HANGING UNDERNEATH the waterline. The semibreve rest HANGS UNDERNEATH the line, like the submarine HANGS UNDERNEATH the waterline.

LOOK and THINK before you count:

- Here are four bars.
- The top number of the time signature indicates four counts in each bar.
- In the first and third bar, there is a semibreve lasting through four counts.
- In the second and last bar, a semibreve rest is hanging underneath the line.

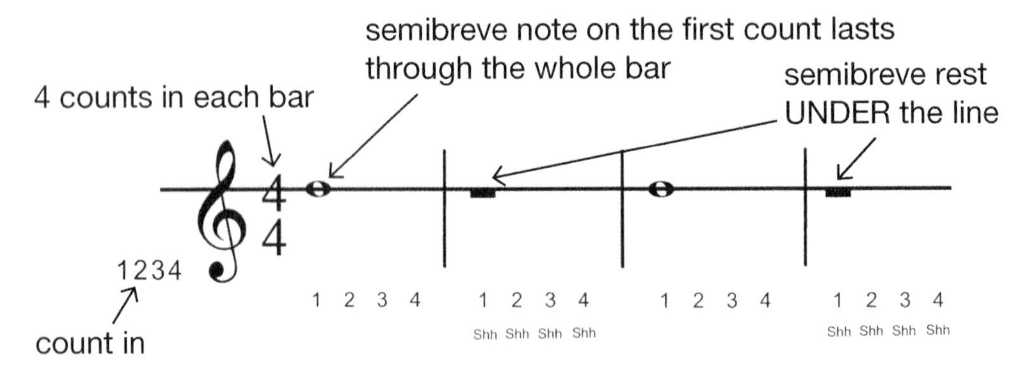

Follow these steps:

- FEEL and sense a slow pulse before you begin.
- COUNT in, and TAP each number with your finger as you LOOK and follow the notes and rests as they go by.
- Either THINK 'shh, shh, shh, shh' OR WHISPER as you count the rests.

Count two bars aloud

Here are some exercises for you to count. Take each one slowly in turn.

Follow the steps through as shown on the previous pages to develop good practising habits. Prepare well. THINK the information through, and FEEL a sensory awareness of the pulse before you start.

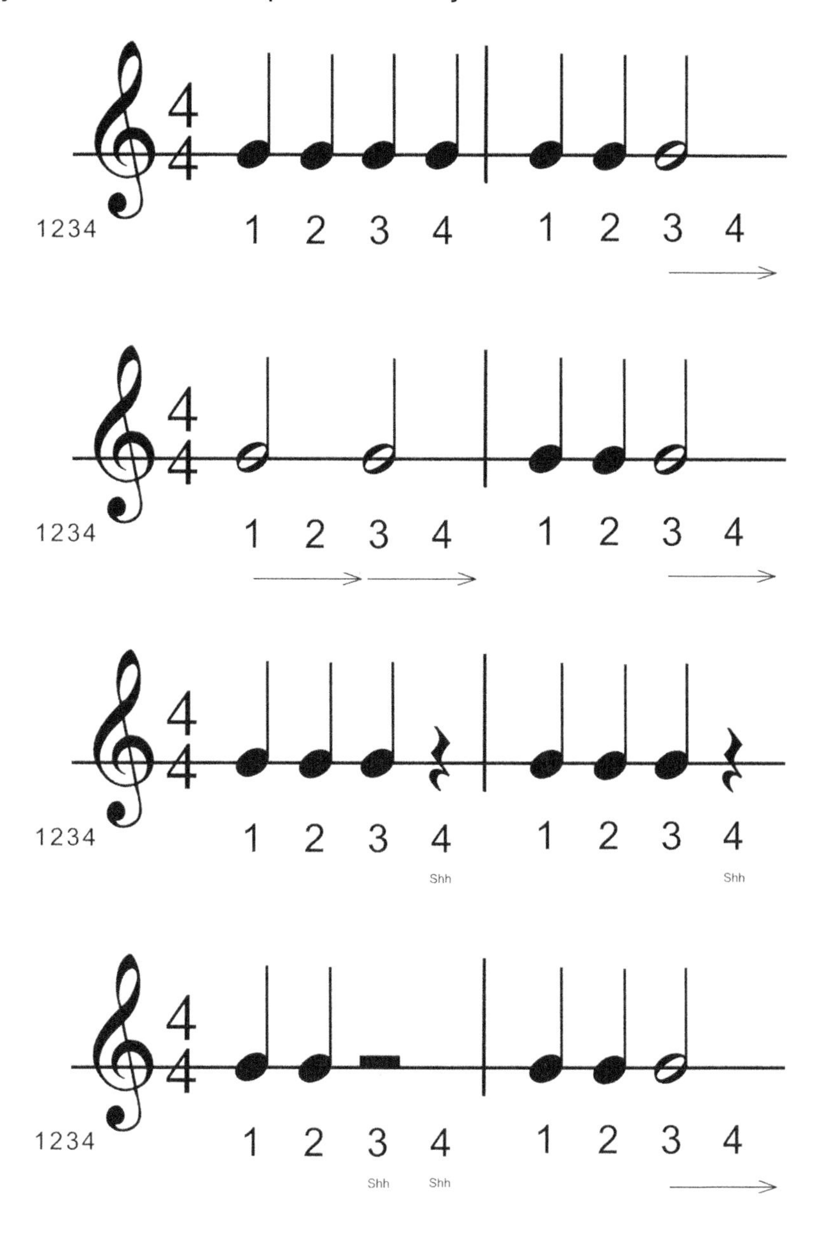

Count four bars aloud

Count each exercise confidently. Make sure you **fit the counting with an even pulse**. Make sure that your **finger taps the number underneath the note** as you count.

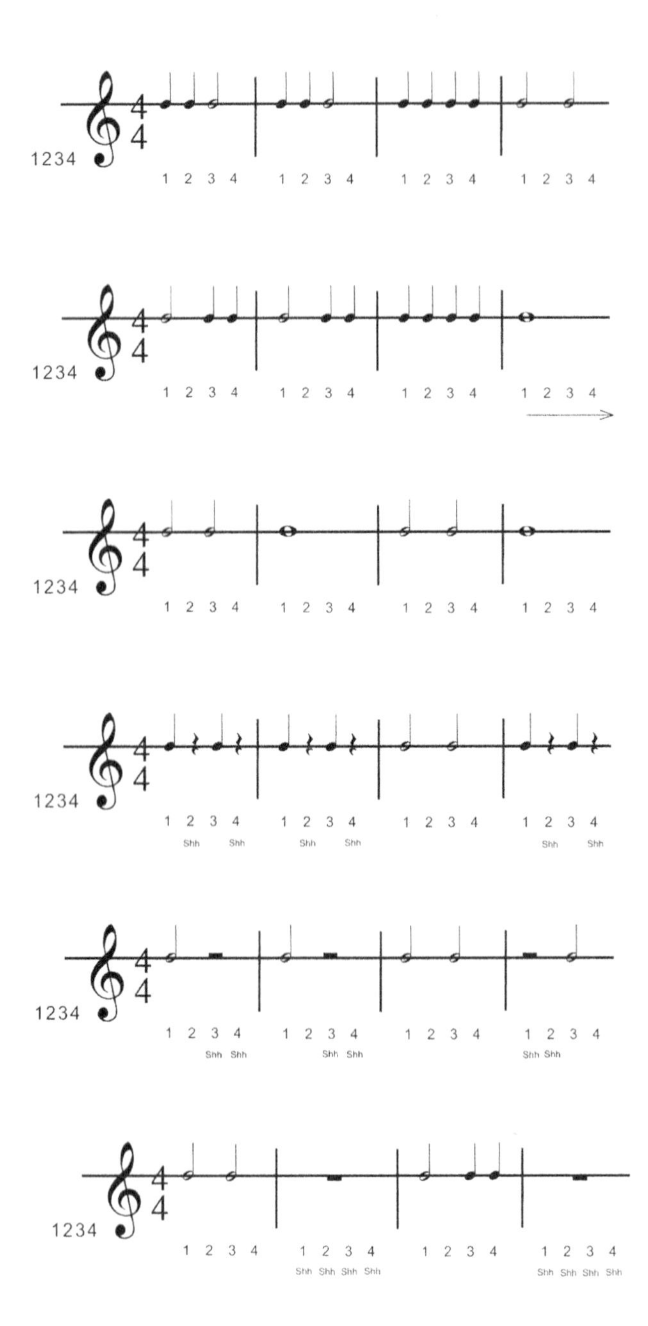

Write the Counting & Mark Your Answers

Use a pencil to write the counting underneath the notes then turn the page and check your answers. Write the 'count in' in the space before the notes start.

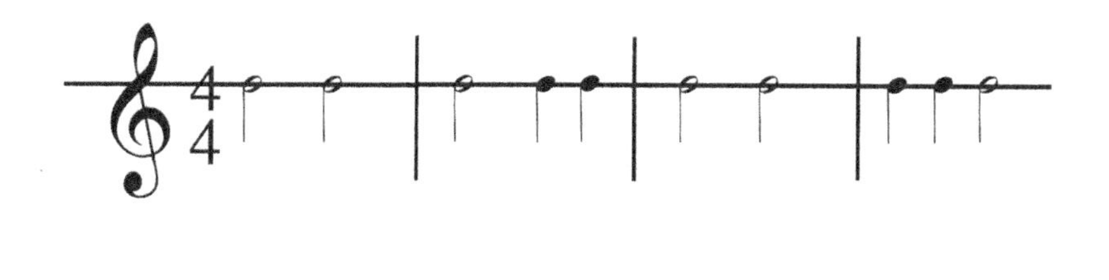

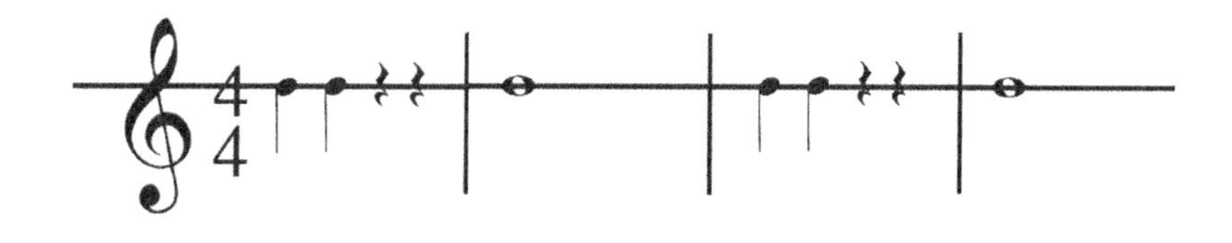

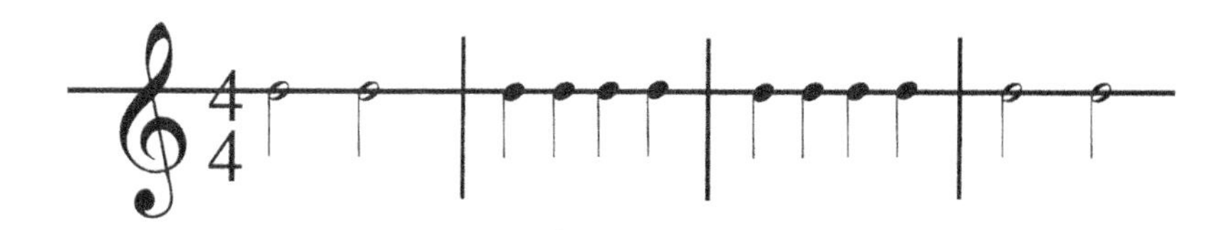

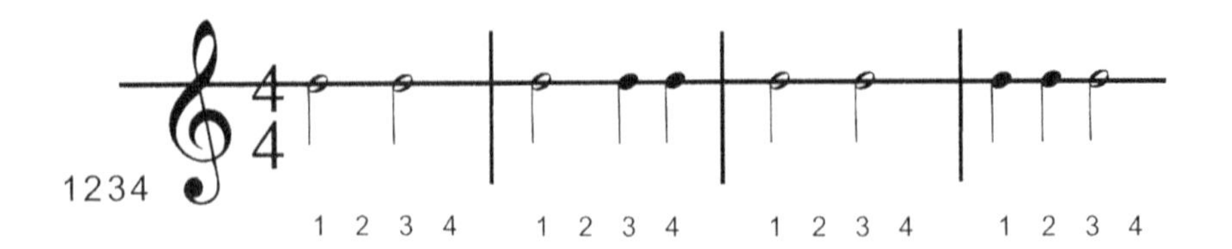

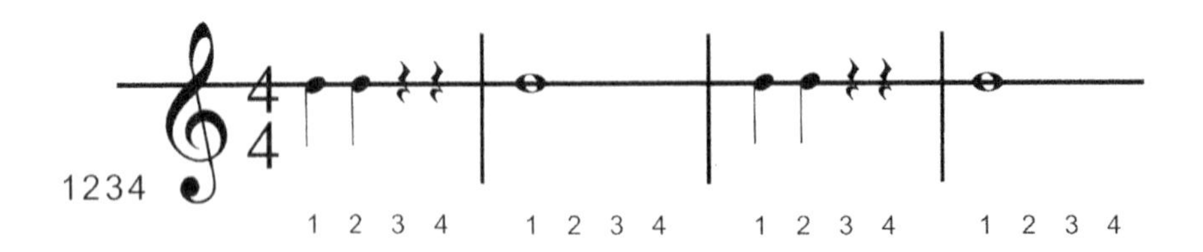

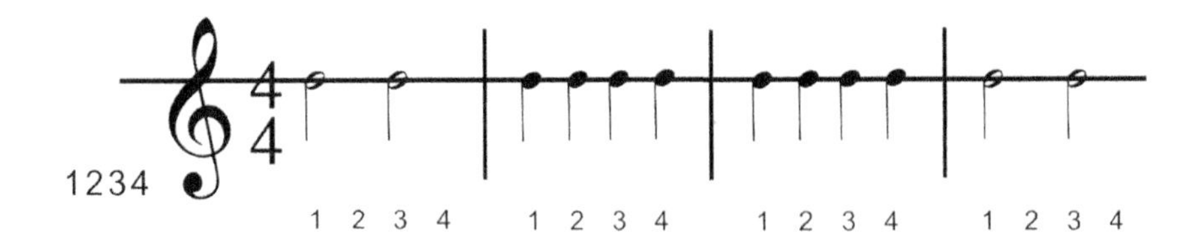

Did you get all the answers right? Now have a go at counting the rhythms out loud.

If you have made a few mistakes in this exercise, go back and read the last few pages again. Learning to apply the instructions practically may take time but with a little patience and practice you will soon grasp the concept of counting the notes to the pulse. In the next chapter, you will apply the same counting principles as you play your clarinet and count silently in your head.

Well Done!

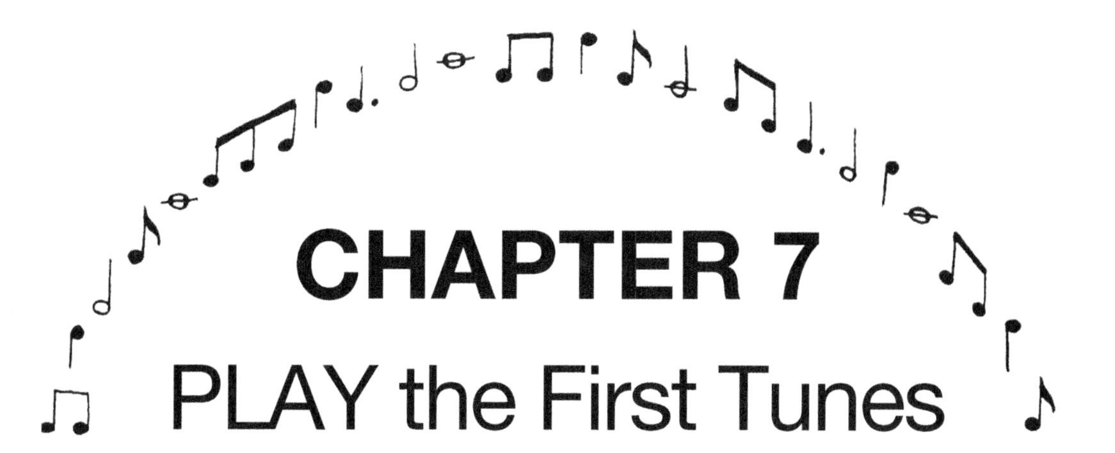

CHAPTER 7

PLAY the First Tunes

Ready to Play?

This chapter will show you what to look for in the music and suggest ways to approach the playing.

- This is ‘Easy Peasy Forever’
- Ready to ‘Swing With D’?
- Get up and ‘March With C’
- Always play ‘Smoothly Please’

Check out ‘Our First Tunes’ in ‘Clarinet Kickstart’ to play along with the accompaniments of the tunes in this chapter
visit www.ClarinetBeginnersCourse.co.uk

This is 'Easy Peasy Forever'

Look and **THINK through the information** on the part:

- There are four bars divided by bar lines. The double bar line at the end tells us that's the end of the piece.
- All the notes sit on the bottom line of the stave. That is the line on which the note 'E' is written. That's 'E' for Easy Peasy! The fingering for 'E' is the first finger and the thumb of the left hand – how easy is that?
- The top number in the time signature tells us that there are four counts in each bar.

- There is a 'count in' of 4 beats at the beginning.

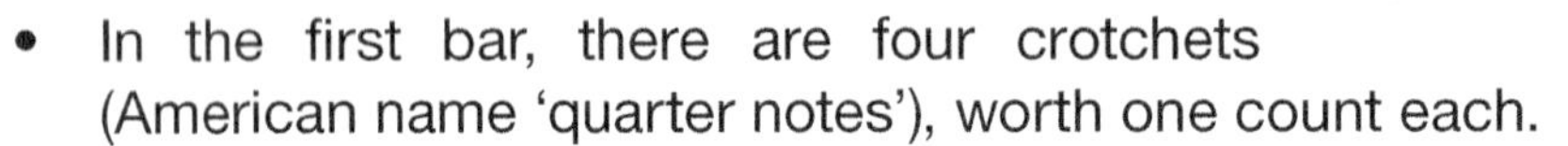

- In the first bar, there are four crotchets (American name 'quarter notes'), worth one count each.

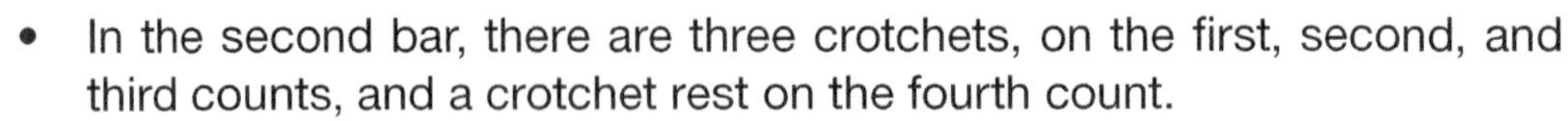

- In the second bar, there are three crotchets, on the first, second, and third counts, and a crotchet rest on the fourth count.
- In the third bar, there are two crotchets on the first and second counts and two crotchet rests on the third and fourth counts.
- In the fourth bar, there are two minims (American name 'half notes') lasting two counts each. The first is on the first beat of the bar, lasting through the first and second beats. The second is on the third beat of the bar lasting through the third and fourth beats.

Easy Peasy Forever

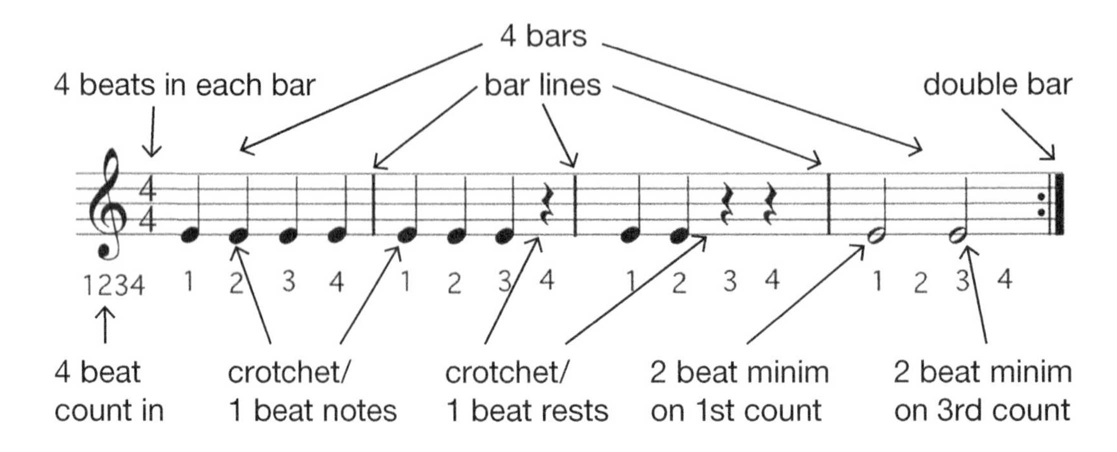

Warm up:

- Finger the note 'E' on the clarinet and play a few strong long notes 'E'.
- Play the same long note but tongue it repeatedly to make a series of 'E' notes. You are effectively chopping up the column of air with the tongue. The notes are joined with no gaps.

FEEL and sense the pulse inside:

- Choose a sensible moderate pace.
- Count 4 beats in and count the notes out loud as you point to the numbers underneath.

Let's play:

- Look at the **first bar.** Imagine pushing a long column of air through its whole length. Count 4 beats in and tongue the four notes lasting the air through to the end.
- Play the **second bar** lasting the air through the three notes and think 'shh' as you count the rest at the end.
- Look at the **third bar.** Count a bar in and count as you play. Tongue the two notes then think 'shh, shh' as you count the rests on 3, 4.
- Now for the **fourth bar.** Remind yourself you will tongue the notes on the first and third counts. Count 4 in, in your head, and play the two minims, lasting the air till the end.
- Play the whole tune. Only breathe at the ends of the bars. Do not make gaps between the notes. Think 'shh' when you count a rest.

Remember

- Your left hand is at the top of the clarinet.
- Your right thumb is straight, under the thumb rest.
- Your clarinet is held out, away from the body.
- You breathe in through the sides of the mouth.

Ready to ‘Swing With D’?

Ready to **THINK through the information?** What do the signs and symbols on the stave mean?

- All the notes appear under the stave. Their name is ‘D’.

  ‘D’ is played with the first two fingers and the thumb of the left hand.
- There are four bars.
- The number 4 at the top of the time signature states four counts in each bar.
- There are two dots at the end, before the double bar. This repeat sign means go back and play the piece again.

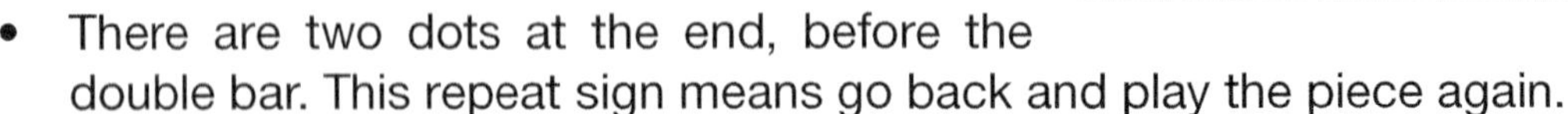

- The notes have different values.

  The minims (American name ‘half notes’) in the first two bars, have a value of two counts each. They last **through** 2 beats.

  The crotchets (American name ‘quarter notes’) in the third bar, have a value of one count each.

  The semibreve (American name ‘whole note’) in the fourth bar, has a value of four counts. It lasts **through** all the four counts in the bar.
- There are minim rests in the first and second bars. These are on the third count. They have a value of two beats, making them last **through** both the third and the fourth counts.

Swing With D

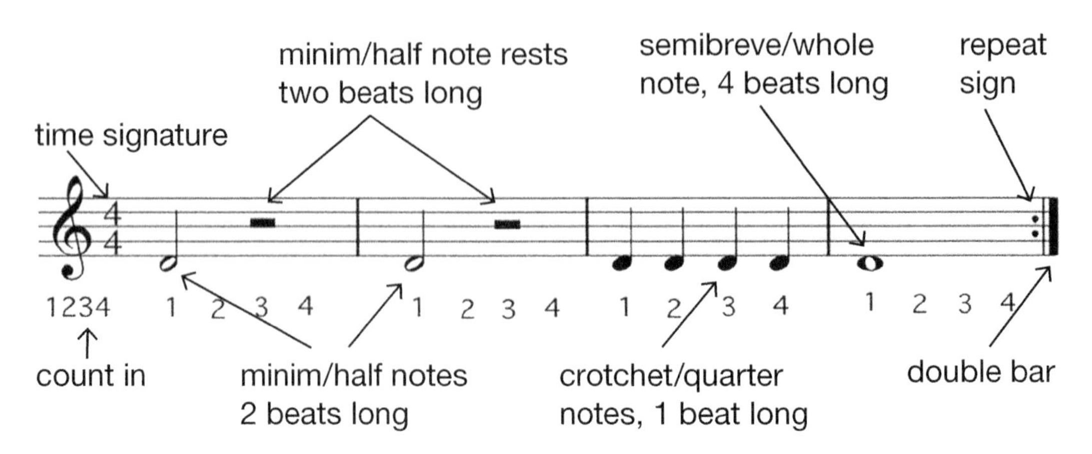

Warm up:

- Revise the fingering for 'D' and play a couple of long, controlled 'D' notes. Recognise you are pushing one long column or sausage shape of air **through** the long note.
- Tongue the reed to make lots of joined up 'D' notes. Make certain that you are not pushing individual puffs of air into the clarinet to make the different notes.

FEEL and sense the pulse inside you:

- Choose a slow speed.
- Count yourself in. Count the rhythm out loud as you point to the numbers underneath the notes. Fit the counting with the pulse.

Let's play:

- Put the clarinet in your mouth and prepare your embouchure.
- Play the first two bars. Count 4 beats in, in your head, breathe in and tongue the note, holding the air on as you count '1, 2,' **through** the note then count '3, 4,' **through** the rest. Think 'shh, shh' as you count the rests too. Make your counting fit with the pulse you feel.
- Play the last two bars together - Count in, in your head, and tongue the reed as you play **through** the two bars making sure the last note is held on for the full four counts.
- Play all the tune all through.

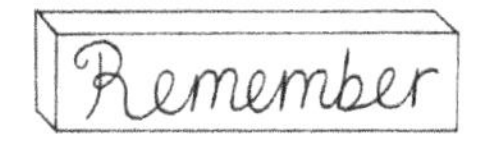

- Tongue all the notes.
- Take air in through the **sides** of the mouth. Do not suck air up through the clarinet or breathe in through the nose.
- The magic word is '**through**' which is why it is highlighted. The air column pushes **through** the clarinet. The notes and the rests are held **through** their length – don't clip the lengths.

Get up and 'March With C'

THINK – read all the information on the stave:

- All the notes are named 'C'. The note appears below the stave sitting on a ledger line. 'C' is played with the first three fingers and the thumb of the left hand.
- There are four bars with four beats in each bar.
- There are two dots at the end, before the double bar. This repeat sign indicates to go back to the beginning and play the piece again.
- All the notes have a value of one count. They are crotchets/quarter notes.
- There are crotchet rests on the fourth count of the bars 1, 2, and 4.

March With C

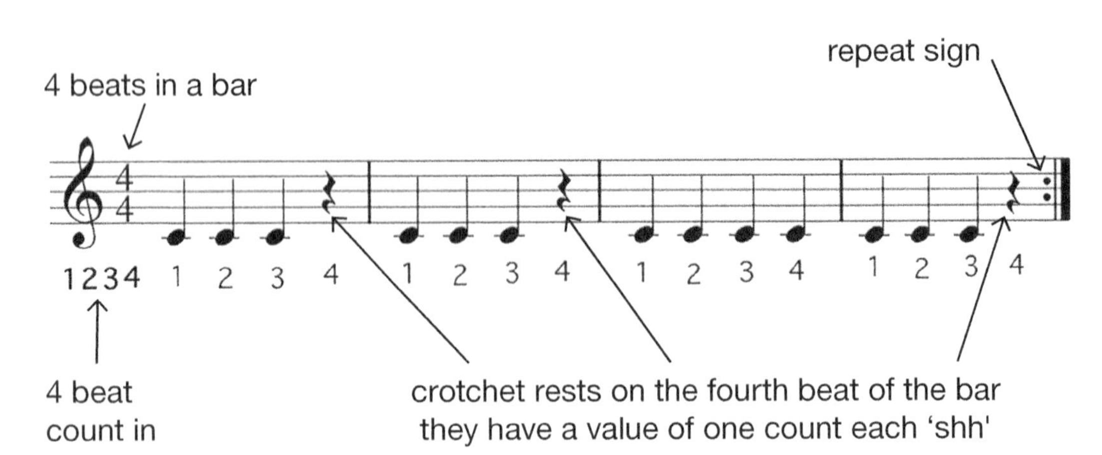

Warm up:

- Revise the 'C' fingering. Play a few long notes to get used to the feeling of the fingers firmly covering the holes and the feeling of the mouth position as you play this note.
- Keep the air even and repeatedly tongue the reed to make many joined up 'C' notes. Think about the sensation of the tip of the tongue as it lightly bounces off the reed, just underneath the tip.

FEEL the pulse:

- Stand up and march on the spot for a few steps. Feel the regular physical movement and how even the steps are. You are setting the pulse.
- Look at the tune, count four beats in and point to the numbers underneath the stave as you count aloud. In this sense, you have your 'finger on the pulse'.

Let's play:

- Play the first two bars. Push the air **through** as you tongue the three 'C' notes. Think 'shh' as you count the rests.
- Play bars 3 and 4 together. Push the sausage of air **through** to the last note making no gaps. If you can't last the air through the two bars that is ok for now. Breathe in at the end of the first.
- Play the whole tune making sure you keep the reed resting on the bottom lip and the top teeth on the mouthpiece as you breathe in.

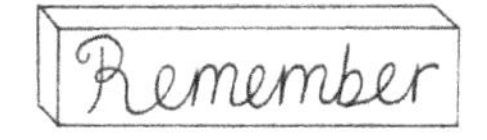

- Be aware of the pulse sensation inside you as you play.
- Make sure all the three fingers fully cover the holes to get the note 'C' easily.
- Count yourself in, in your head, every time you play.
- Make sure you are not touching the side key under the first finger. This may cause a squeak!

Always play 'Smoothly Please'

THINK! – Absorb all the information on the stave first!

- There are three different notes in this tune: 'E', 'D', and 'C'.
- There are eight bars in this piece.
- The time signature indicates four beats in each bar.
- There are breath marks at the end of each two bars, indicated by a tick.
- The notes are mostly one beat crotchets with a value of one count.
- There are minim notes, with a value of two counts in bars four and eight. These notes are held **through** two counts.

Smoothly Please

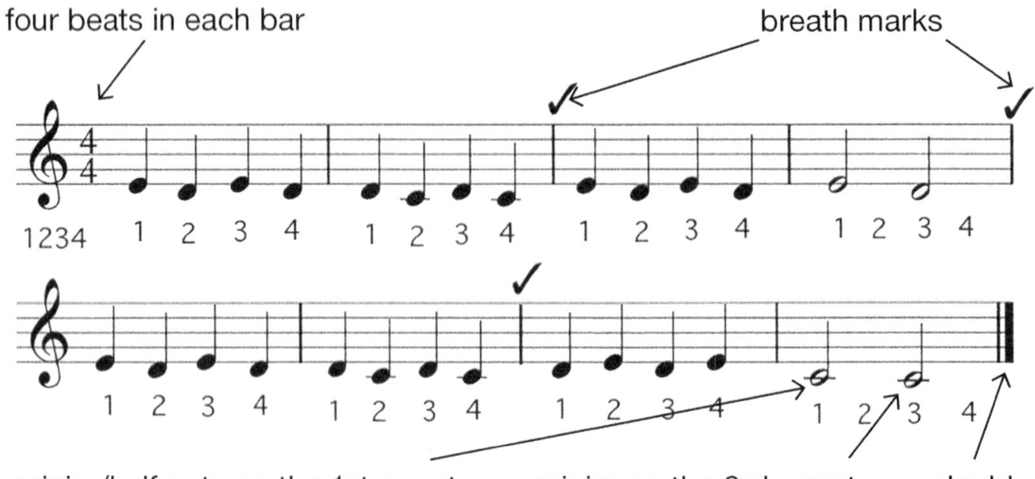

Warm up:

- Play 'E', 'D', 'E', 'D', 'E', 'D', 'E', 'D', until the second finger moves fluently and smoothly on and off the second hole. Make sure it seals the second hole completely. Keep all the fingers rounded and near to the clarinet. Make no gaps between the notes. Count in before you do this exercise so you play to a pulse. You will then play 'rhythmically'.
- Play 'D', 'C', 'D', 'C', 'D', 'C', 'D', 'C'. Play exactly to the even pulse you are feeling. Work the third finger until it moves fluently on and off the hole and seals it every single time. Do not lift the finger high in the air as you take it off the hole. Tongue every single note.

Set and **FEEL a slow pulse**

- Count the tune through to learn the movement of the notes.

Let's play:

- Notice bars 1, 3 and 5 are the same. Play the first bar. Count yourself in, in your head, and tongue the notes to articulate them.
- Notice bars 2 and 6 are the same. Play the second bar.
- Play the first two bars on their own. **Try to last the air through the two bars** – from the first note of the first bar through to the final note of the second bar.
- Learn the rest of the tune in two bar sections.
- Play the whole piece through. Breathe at the end of each two bars as indicated. If you cannot manage to hold the breath through two bars at present that is fine for now. In this case, breathe in at the ends of the bars – not in the middle of the bars.

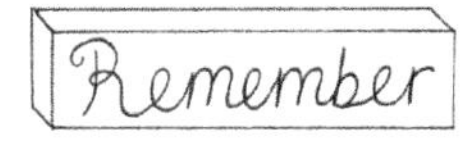

- Push the air column through the two bars evenly. Do not stop the air, as restarting the air mid bar spoils the flow of the music.
- Understand that pushing a column of air through 8 one beat notes is precisely the same as pushing a column of air through one note for eight counts.

CHAPTER 8
LEARN the Next Signs and Symbols

- Dynamics
- Speed Words
- Slur Marks and How to Slur
- More Repeats
- More About Time Signatures
- How About Key Signatures?

When you've gained the ability to play the first few notes, sensed the pulse and worked with the core note values, you'll discover many new signs and symbols in the written parts which can make the music sound so much more attractive and appealing – these suggest various exciting ways through which you can express your musicianship.

Music signs and symbols are all simplistic individually – but having to follow too many instructions at once could be a challenge for any beginner. It's wise to explore and understand these signs and symbols, one at a time, before applying them to your playing.

Dynamics

It would be rather boring to hear a piece of music played at the same volume for the whole duration. By adding variations of loud and soft, you can increase the appeal of a piece immeasurably.

In music, the word 'Dynamic' usually refers to the level of loudness and softness in the piece.

The words used to describe the levels of loud and soft are Italian words. Their abbreviations always appear below the stave, if possible, directly underneath the notes to which they are referring. A dynamic mark lasts through the music until the next change of dynamic – if any.

The basic dynamic instructions used are: 'f', meaning play loudly, 'p', meaning play softly and 'm', indicating 'moderately'. Memorise these three abbreviations then both the chart below and the dynamic instructions in your pieces will make sense to you.

Abbreviation	Meaning	Italian word
p	Soft	Piano
pp	Very soft	Pianissimo
f	Loud	Forte
ff	Very loud	Fortissimo
mp	Moderately soft	Mezzo-piano
mf	Moderately loud	Mezzo-forte

'Crescendo' means gradually play louder, so we increase the volume over the duration of the crescendo. The sign looks like a hair pin, and so it's sometimes called a hair pin! It appears underneath a series of notes indicating to gradually get louder from the first note through to the last.

The 'Decrescendo' sign means gradually get softer from the first note to the last. Another word for 'decrescendo' is 'diminuendo'.

Speed Words

There are special words to indicate the speed of the music which are also Italian. They are written above the top of the stave usually on the left, after the treble clef sign and around the time signature area.

There are many traditional Italian speed words, but it is not necessary to know them all at the beginning. The important ones to know are:

Allegro - quickly
Moderato - moderately
Andante - walking speed
Lento - slowly

Modern day composers may not use the traditional Italian words to describe speed. You will find some modern pieces using English words – 'quick', 'moderate', 'slow' etc.

Slur Marks and How to Slur

A curved line either above or below a group of different notes indicates a slur. Slurred notes are not tongued. They join to each other and sound 'legato' which means 'smooth'.

In the first period of playing, we may tongue all the notes to get used to the light movement of the tip of the tongue, as it bounces off the reed to articulate the notes. Once this essential habit establishes itself, it is then easy to appreciate the physical sensation between slurring a note and tonguing it.

Slurring on the clarinet is easy. Take your instrument and slur ‘E’ to ‘D’ to ‘C’. Cover the first hole and thumb hole with the left-hand finger and thumb. Tongue the 'E' note, then without stopping the air, put the second and third fingers down in turn. You have slurred the notes together! Notice the different sensation as you allow the air to flow through the clarinet as you put your fingers down without tonguing.

Do not confuse a slur line with a tie. A line that joins two notes of the same pitch is called a 'tie', which simply 'ties' the values of the two notes together to make a longer note. A slur line joins notes that are different.

Rule:
If a note is not joined to the previous note with a slur line, it is tongued.

If a note joins to the last note with a slur line it is slurred.

In this example, the tongue articulates the first note of the first three bars and both the notes in the last bar. All the other notes are slurred.

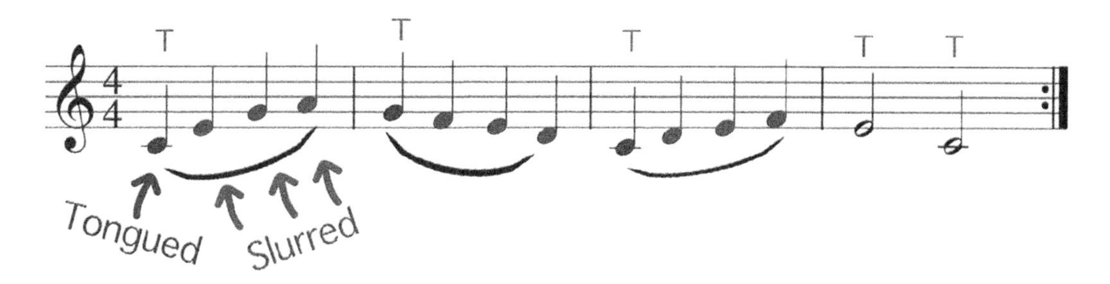

- In the first bar, the first note is not tied to a previous note, therefore, it is tongued.
- The next three notes in the bar tie to the previous note, so they are slurred.
- In bar four, both the notes are tongued.

Practise correct 'articulation'.

The word to describe the tonguing and slurring collectively is 'articulation'. When we tongue the reed we 'articulate' it to produce the sound. When the teacher says "please 'articulate' correctly", it has a slightly different implication, meaning observe both the tonguing and the slurring as is written when you play the piece.

Articulate correctly from the very beginning!

It takes some special focus and attention to make correct articulation habitual, but once you tongue and slur as a matter of course, you'll agree that it is easy. Many beginners develop a habit of slurring everything because it seems easier not to use the tongue at first. The result is then sloppy playing, which has no shape.

Take time and apply patience to 'articulate' correctly from the start, as it will be a challenge to discipline a change later.

More Repeats

You are already familiar with the two-dot repeat sign before the double bar which means 'play it again'. However, there are additional repeats that enable the composer to send the player to different parts of the piece to play a section again as opposed to just the beginning.

Sometimes, musicians refer to the 'geography' of the piece. That means where the music goes, in sequence, with respect to the various repeats. It is sensible to 'sort out the geography' of the piece before starting to play, so your eye can find the repeats easily and quickly.

Repeat from the Beginning

The repeat sign at the end of the fourth bar means to repeat from the start and play the section again.

Repeat from the Previous Repeat Sign.

Above you can see a repeat sign within the double bar at the beginning of bar five. At the end of the last bar, the repeat goes back to this repeat sign in bar five.

So, the 'geography' of the piece is...

From the beginning play through to the end of bar four then repeat back to the beginning, and at the end of the last bar repeat back to bar five and play to the end.

RULE:
If there is no repeat mark to go back to, repeat from the beginning.

If there is a repeat mark at the start of a bar, repeat from there.

First and Second Time Bars.

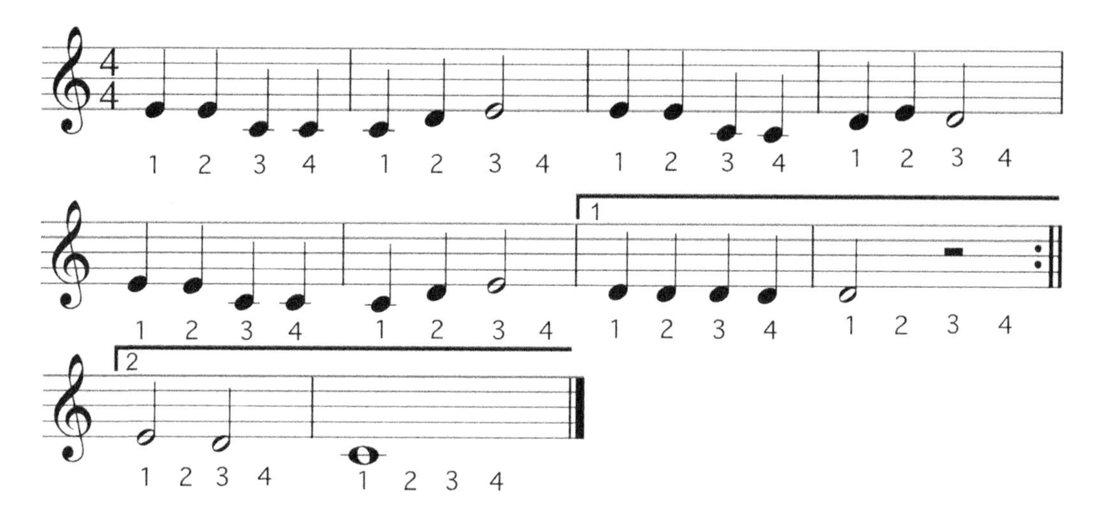

There is a bracket which goes over bars 7 and 8 indicating the 'First-Time Bar' (see the small number '1'). The first-time bar is played on the first time through. The last two bars have a bracket with a small number '2' indicating the 'Second-Time Bar' played on the second time through. On the repeat, the player omits the first-time bar and immediately jumps to the second-time bar to end the piece.

The 'geography' of the piece is then:

- From the beginning play to the end of the first-time bar (bar 8).
- Repeat back to the beginning and at the end of bar 6, omit the first-time bar and jump to the second-time bar.

More About Time Signatures

We have learned tunes with four beats in each bar, written with the time signature of 4/4.

Sometimes this time signature is shown as 'C'. It's then referred to as 'Common Time'. 4/4 and 'Common Time' mean the same.

After the initial stage of learning, you will come across new time signatures. For the beginning period, new players need only be concerned with the top number of the time signature, which indicates the number of beats in each bar. Some tunes have two beats in a bar; some have three and others have even more than that.

4/4 3/4 2/2

In later playing you will need to understand the meaning of the lower number so this is how it's done.

The **top number** of the time signature states **the number of beats per bar**.

The lower number indicates the **value of those beats i.e. what kind of beats they are.**

Table of Note Values

Note	English name	Value	American Name	Rest
𝅝	Semibreve	4 beats	Whole note	
𝅗𝅥	Minim	2 beats	Half note	
♩	Crotchet	1 beat	Quarter note	
♪	Quaver	1/2 beat	Eighth note	

To interpret the lower number of a time signature look at the American Names in the chart.

The American name for the semibreve, with a value of four beats, is a 'whole note', for a two beat minim, it's a 'half note', 1/2, for a one beat crotchet, it's a 'quarter note', 1/4, and for the half beat quaver, the American name is an 'eighth note', 1/8.

Knowing the American names helps us to understand the meaning of the bottom number of the time signature which indicates the value of the beat.

A number 4 at the bottom means the value of the beat is a **quarter note**. That is the same as a Crotchet.

A number 2 at the bottom means the value of the beat is a **half note**. That is the same as a Minim.

A number 8 at the bottom means the value of the beat is an **eighth note**. That is the same as a Quaver.

Four four time

Note	English name	Value	American Name
𝅝	Semibreve	4 beats	Whole note
𝅗𝅥	Minim	2 beats	Half note
♩	Crotchet	1 beat	Quarter note
♪	Quaver	1/2 beat	Eighth note

4 ← How many beats per bar
4 ← What kind of notes

The top number here tells us there are four beats in each bar. The lower number indicates that the value of the beat is a quarter note/crotchet. There are four quarter notes per bar.

Four beats to the value of a quarter note/crotchet is known as 'four four time'.

Three four time

Note	English name	Value	American Name
𝅝	Semibreve	4 beats	Whole note
𝅗𝅥	Minim	2 beats	Half note
♩	Crotchet	1 beat	Quarter note
♪	Quaver	1/2 beat	Eighth note

3 ↙ How many beats per bar
4 ↙ What kind of notes

Here the top number is a 3. The lower number 4, indicates that the value of the beat is a quarter note/crotchet.

Three beats in a bar to the value of a crotchet is known a 'three four time'.

Two two time

Note	English name	Value	American Name
𝅝	Semibreve	4 beats	Whole note
𝅗𝅥	Minim	2 beats	Half note
♩	Crotchet	1 beat	Quarter note
♪	Quaver	1/2 beat	Eighth note

2 ↙ How many beats per bar
2 ↙ What kind of notes

Number 2 at the top means two beats in each bar. The lower number 2 means the value of the beat is a half note. That is the same thing as a minim.

A time signature of 2/2, means two beats to the value of a minim and is known as 'two two time'.

Playing in the time of 2/2 gives the music a much lighter feel than when playing in 4/4, which could be interpreted as the same thing – however, this is for the concern of the advanced player. It is quite sufficient and desirable to pay attention to only the top number of the time signature – the number of beats in the bar – during the first stages of learning.

How About Key Signatures?

The Key Signature is recognized as several sharps or flats written at the beginning of the line of music. It declares the sharpening or flattening of certain notes within the piece. It's always situated after the treble clef sign and before the time signature.

When the pitch of a note rises by a semitone, which is a small step, it is 'sharpened'. When it is lowered by a semitone, it is 'flattened'.

The Key Signature of One Sharp

The sharp sign sits on the top line of the stave. Notice that the line goes right through the middle of the sharp sign.

Recall the names of the notes on the lines by saying the line 'Every Good Boy Deserves Football'.

The top line is the line on which the note 'F' is written. The sharp sign sitting here, tells us that all the notes named 'F' now become 'F#' irrespective of whether they are low 'F's or high 'F's. The 'F' notes are raised, they are sharpened, and they now become 'F#'.

The Key Signature of One Flat

The flat sign sits on the middle line of the stave.

Remembering the line 'Every Good Boy...' tells us that the name of the notes on the middle line is 'B'.

A flat sign on the 'B' line says that all the 'B' notes are now 'Bb'. The 'B' notes are lowered in pitch. They now become 'Bb'.

The Key Signature of Two Sharps

The first sharp in a key signature is always 'F'. The sharp sign sits ON the top line indicating that all the 'F' notes are now 'F#'.

The second sharp sign sits IN the third space up. Notice the difference in appearance between the sharp sign sitting ON the line and the sharp sign sitting IN the space.

Recall that spelling the word 'FACE' upwards from the bottom indicates the names of the notes in the spaces.

The sharp sign sits IN the 'C' space. All the 'C' notes now become 'C#'.

The Key Signature of Two Flats

The first flat in a key signature is always 'B'. It's indicated by the flat sign sitting ON the middle line.

The second flat sits IN the top space of the stave flattening all the notes named 'E'.

In your studies; you will first learn tunes with either one or two sharps or flats in the key signature. You will encounter more over time, as you learn to play in other keys.

You will appreciate that it is important to observe the key signature before you start playing. It is wise to quickly look through the part to see the notes that are affected by it, then you will be prepared to sharpen or flatten the notes accordingly.

CHAPTER 9

COUNT Quaver Rhythms and Dotted Notes

Here we go with the 'Eighth':

- Quick Quaver Reminder
- How to Count Quaver Notes
- Let's Get Counting!
- Write the Counting and Mark your Answers

Now for the 'Dots':

- Getting to the Point – What is a Dotted Note?
- The Easy Counting of Dotted Notes
- Check Out Your Understanding

To get the most benefit from this chapter, make sure you are familiar with all the content and exercises in Chapter 6, 'Count the First Rhythms'. Feel comfortable with both the reading method shown and the interpretation and understanding of Crotchets, Minims, and Semibreves and their rests.

Quick Quaver Reminder

Chapter 5, 'LEARN the first Signs and Symbols', touched only briefly on the quaver note, so some quick revision of this note value is in place here.

The American name for the quaver is an 'eighth', because it is an eighth of a whole note. There are two quavers in a crotchet.

When the quaver stands on its own, it appears as a black note with a stem and a flag.

Two quavers together are joined with one line at the top or the bottom. Sometimes quavers are grouped in 4's or more. Regardless of how they are grouped, they are always joined with one line.

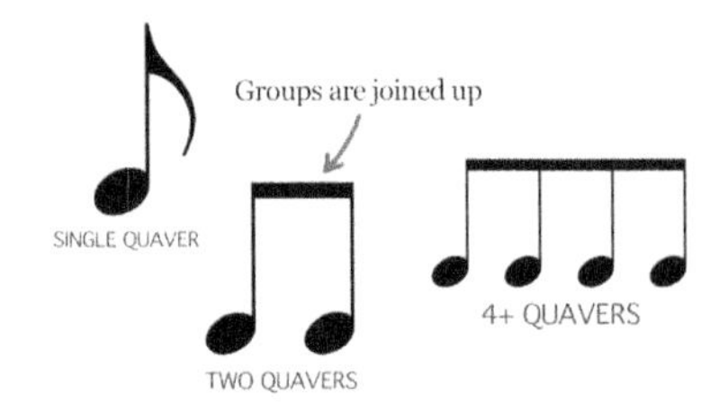

The quaver rest looks a little like a number 7.

Note	English name	Value	American Name	Rest
𝅝	Semibreve	4 beats	Whole note	
𝅗𝅥	Minim	2 beats	Half note	
♩	Crotchet	1 beat	Quarter note	
♪	Quaver	1/2 beat	Eighth note	

Look how the quaver fits into the note value chart.

Note its appearance, its English name, the note value, its American name and the quaver rest symbol.

How to Count Quaver Notes

When you play quaver notes, be attentive to the special counting of the quaver rhythm.

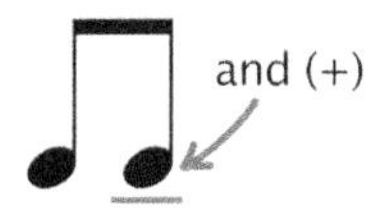

The first quaver of a group of two, sitting ON the beat, is counted by the number of its position in the bar. The second quaver of a group of two comes after the beat. Musicians call this OFF the beat. This second (OFF beat) quaver is always counted as 'and'. That is its name. Musicians write this either as '&' or '+'.

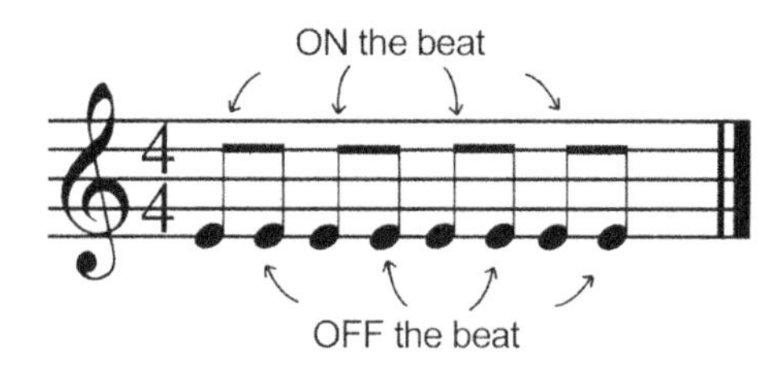

Quaver Counting Example 1

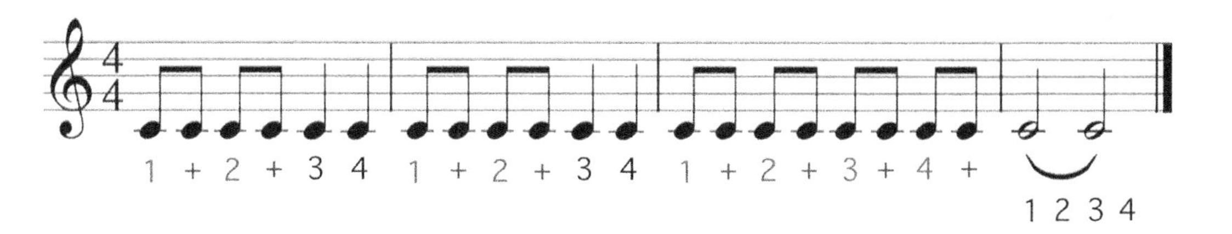

- With the first group of two quavers above, the first note falls ON the first beat, so it is counted as 'one'. The next quaver is still in the space of the first beat. It's on the OFF beat. It is counted as 'and'. The two together are written '1 +' and counted 'one, and'.
- The second two quavers are counted as 'two, and'.
- On beats three and four there are two crotchets counted as 'three, four'.

Do this please Tap four counts, then count aloud 'one and, two and, three, four' to the next taps, and you will feel the rhythm of the quavers and crotchets fitting with the pulse.

- Look at the third bar. There are four groups of two quavers, 'one and, two and, three and, four and'.
- Look at the last bar. There are two minim notes joined with a line which is called a 'tie' (remember, this is not a slur). Ties join notes that are the same pitch. The two notes tied together last through the whole bar.

Quaver Counting Example 2

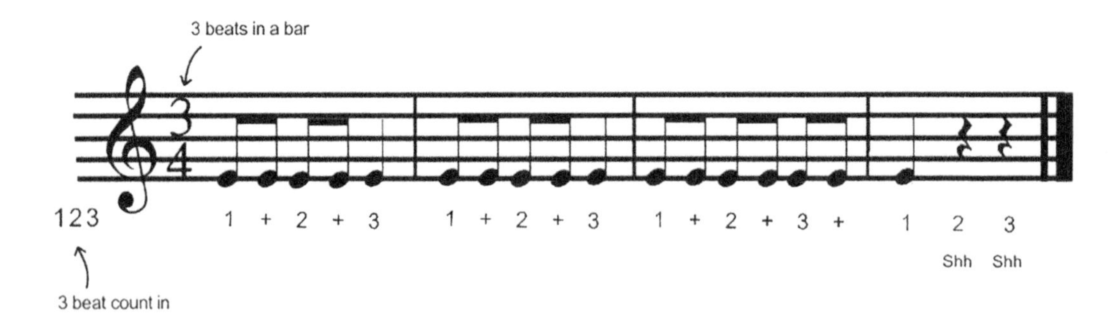

- There are three beats in each bar. The 'count in' will therefore be '1, 2, 3'.
- The first two bars are the same having two sets of quavers and one crotchet, fitting into the three beats of the bar '1&, 2&, 3'. Notice the ON beat and the OFF beat notes.
- In the last bar there is a one beat crotchet on the first count, then two, one beat rests on the second and third. Think 'shh, shh' as you count these rests.

Let's Get Counting!

Here are some phrases to analyse and count yourself. There are various pointers to assist you. Remember the importance of preparing and sensing the pulse. As we learned before, there is simply no point in merely 'thinking' the counting of the rhythm. The 'thinking' must fit with the pulse you sense inside. You are on the way to making music which is vital, rhythmical and alive!

LOOK and THINK through each exercise and notice:

- The time signature, for the number of beats in each bar.
- The 'kind' or 'value' of the notes and rests within the bars.
- Patterns of notes that repeat.
- Any repeat signs.

And again! – follow these guiding steps learned previously:

- FEEL and set a slow pulse.
- COUNT yourself in, and TAP the number underneath the note or rest with your finger as you count aloud. **Don't tap the 'and', just tap the number ON the beat as you count.**
- LOOK and follow the notes as you count.

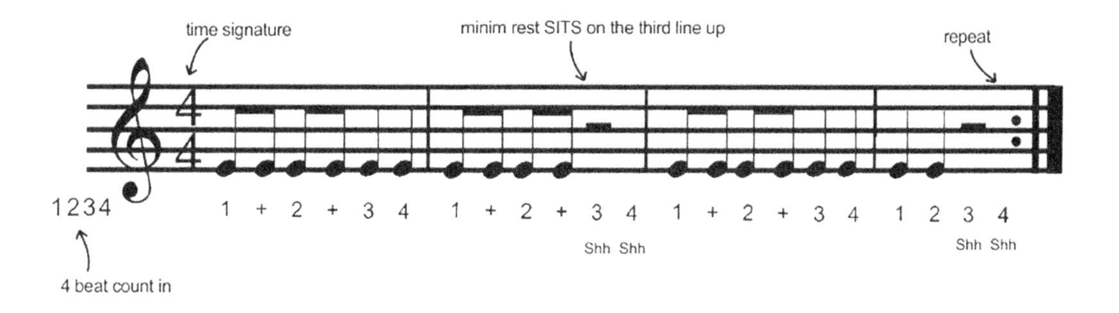

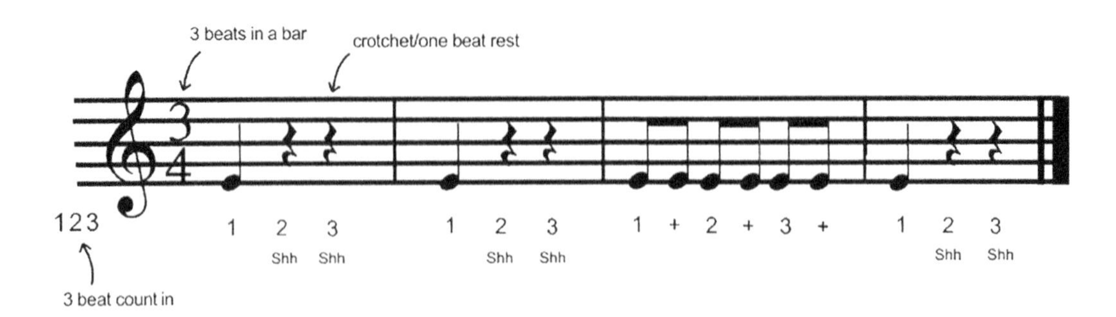
3 beats in a bar
crotchet/one beat rest
123
1 2 3
Shh Shh
1 2 3
Shh Shh
1 + 2 + 3 +
1 2 3
Shh Shh
3 beat count in

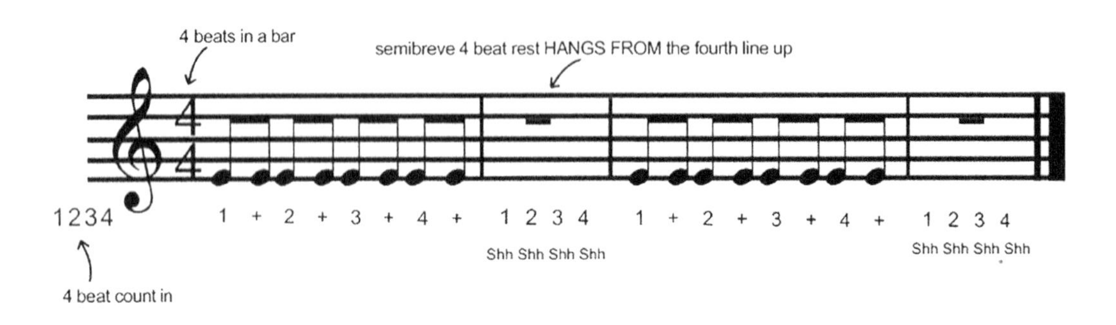
4 beats in a bar
semibreve 4 beat rest HANGS FROM the fourth line up
1234
1 + 2 + 3 + 4 +
1 2 3 4
Shh Shh Shh Shh
1 + 2 + 3 + 4 +
1 2 3 4
Shh Shh Shh Shh
4 beat count in

minim/half note
repeat
123
1 2 3 +
1 2 3
1 2 3 +
1 2 3
3 beat count in

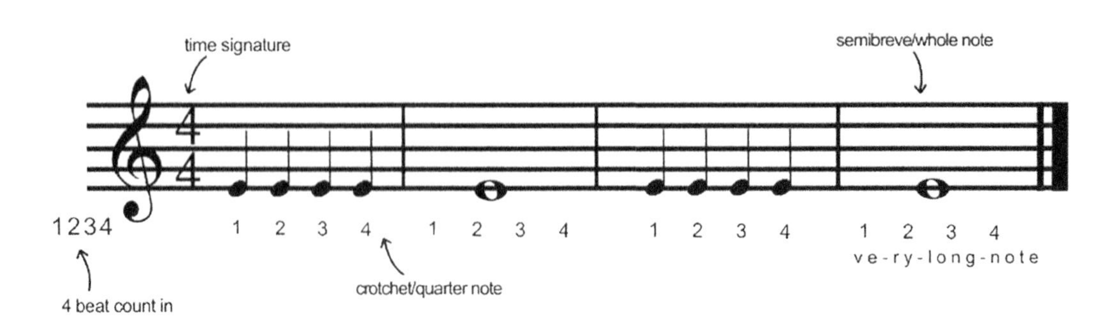
time signature
semibreve/whole note
1234
1 2 3 4
1 2 3 4
1 2 3 4
1 2 3 4
ve-ry-long-note
crotchet/quarter note
4 beat count in

Write the Counting and Mark your Answers

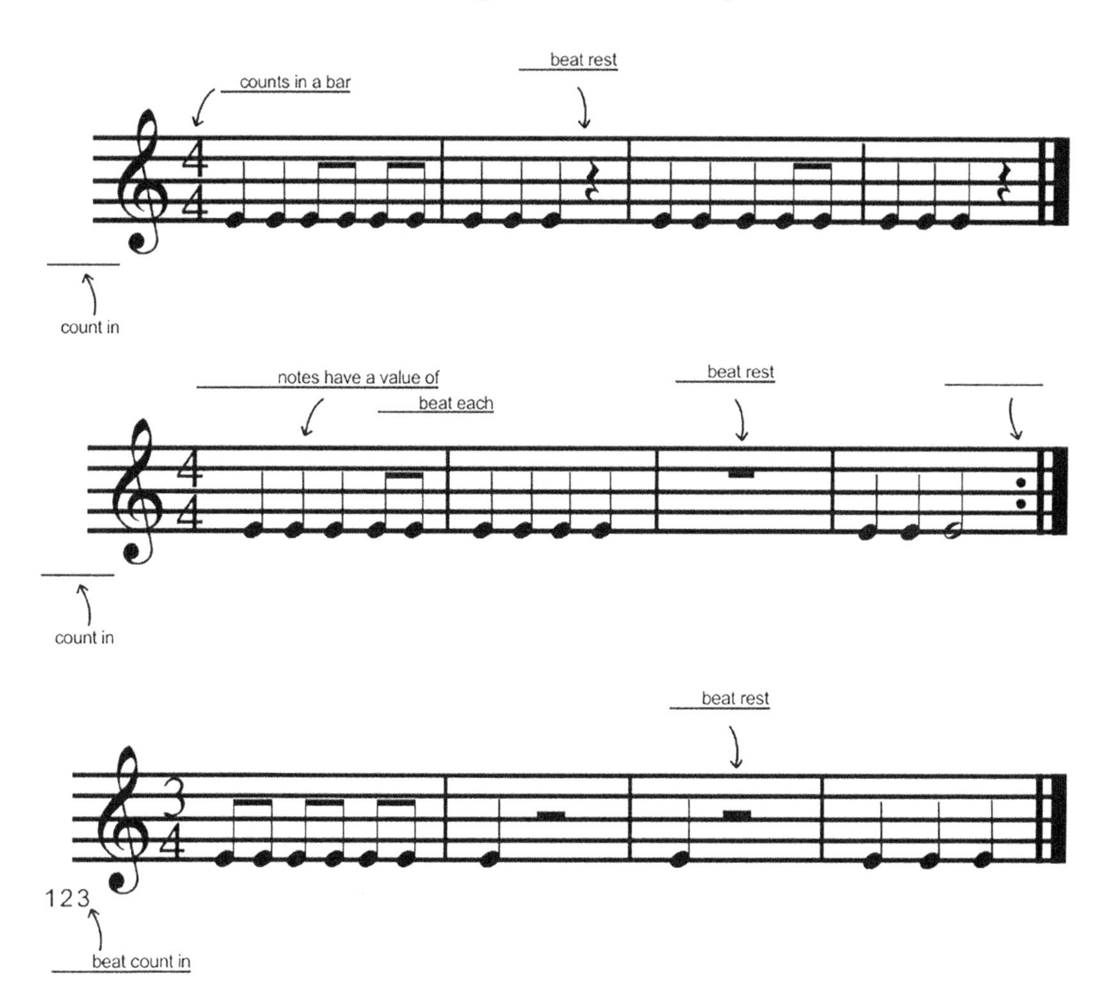

Feel a pulse as you work out the rhythms above.

In pencil:

- Write the counting underneath the notes.
- Write the 'count in', if it is missing.
- Fill in the missing words on the lines.
- Write the 'shh' underneath the rests too.

Turn the page to check your answers ⟶

Mark your answers

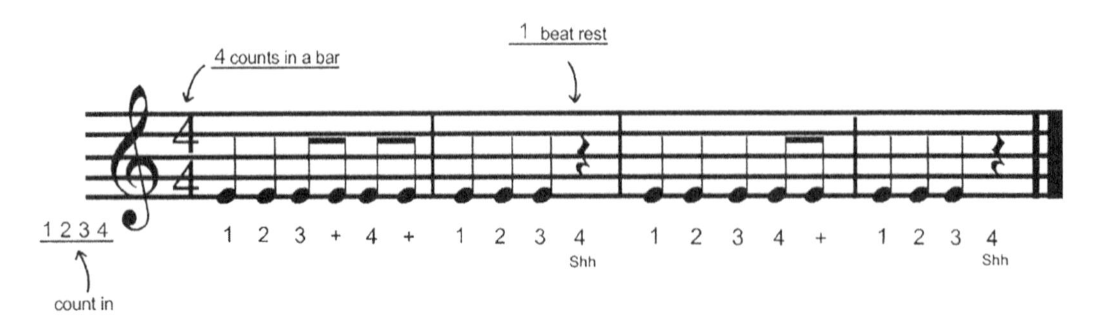

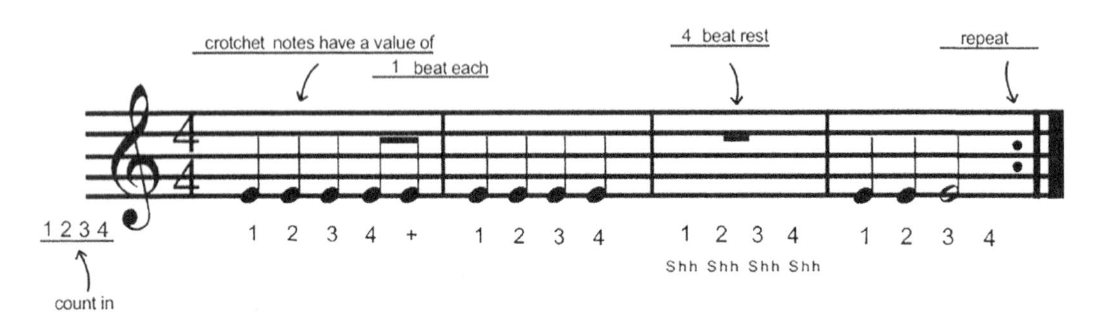

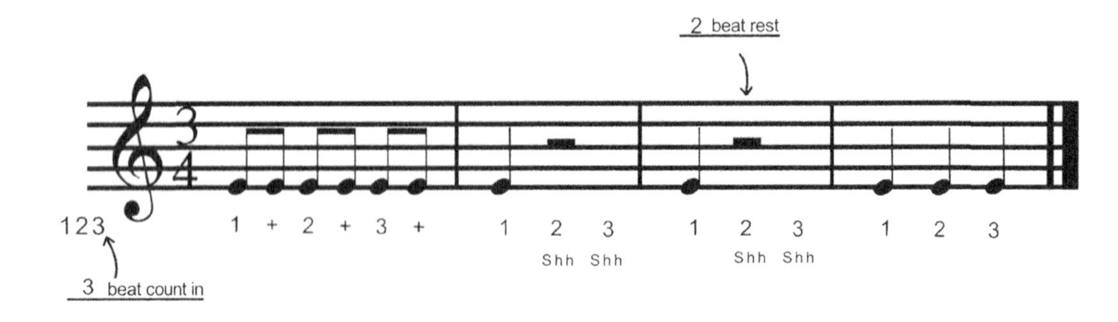

How did you do? If you got many wrong:

- Study the last pages again – or for more thorough revision...
- Read the chapter 'Counting in the First Stages', but more importantly...
- Relax! Beautiful clarinet players evolve beautifully over time! Always enjoy your music!

Getting to the Point – What is a Dotted Note?

A dot placed after a note makes the note longer by half its value.

Dotted minim explained:

- On its own, a minim has a value of two.
- The dot adds half its value.
- Half the value of a minim is one beat. That is the same as a crotchet.

- A dotted minim has the value of a two beat minim and a one beat crotchet added together, making a value of three.

$2 + 1 = 3$

Dotted crotchet explained:

- On its own, the crotchet has a value of one.
- The dot adds half the value.
- Half the value of a crotchet is half a beat. That is the same as a quaver.

- A dotted crotchet has the value of a one beat crotchet and a half beat quaver together making a value of one and a half.

$1 + \frac{1}{2} = 1\frac{1}{2}$

The Easy Counting of Dotted Notes

Beginners usually find the reading and playing of dotted minims comfortable straight away, but sometimes find dotted crotchets a challenge. In fact, all dotted notes are simple to read once you get your head around them. Please follow these few examples through carefully to enable you to play these rhythms well from the start.

Reading the Dotted Minim.

You will find these two examples self-explanatory.

This piece has three beats in each bar.
The dotted minim, with a value of 3 fills the whole of the bar.

Above there are four beats in each bar.

In the first and second bar the dotted minim takes the space of the first three beats. The note is counted through beats one, two and three. On the fourth beat, there is a crotchet.

In the last bar, the dotted minim is the only note in the bar. The fourth beat in the bar is taken up by a one beat rest. Rests are always included in the counting.

Reading the Dotted Crotchet.

The two bars below mean the same.

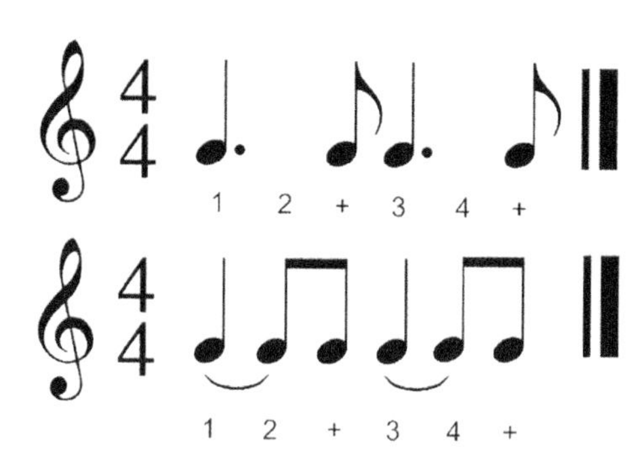

In the lower bar, the first crotchet is tied to a quaver making it 1½ beats long.

Above, the same thing is expressed by a dotted crotchet.

Remember – the second quaver in a group of two is on the OFF beat and always counted as 'and':

- The first note is counted through both the first *and* the second counts.
- The next note, the quaver, is counted as 'and' as it's on the second half of the second beat.
- The dotted crotchet on the third beat is counted through the third *and* fourth beats.
- The last quaver is on the second half of the fourth count. It is on the 'OFF beat' of four.

Count ALOUD through the following rhythms. Notice that in the first example the time signature indicates two beats in each bar.

1 2 +
1 2
1 2 +
1 2

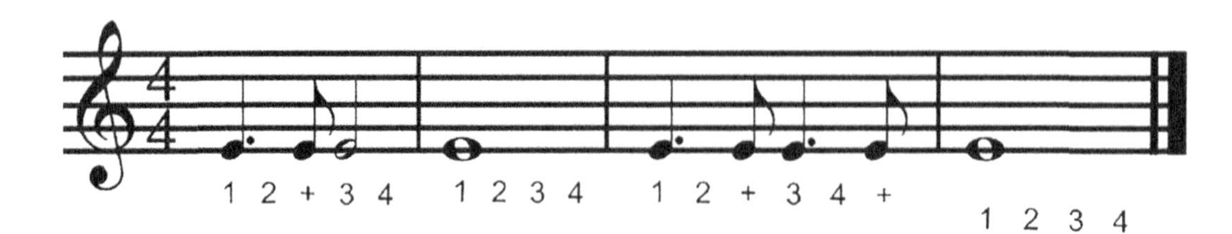
1 2 + 3 4
1 2 3 4
1 2 + 3 4 +
1 2 3 4

1 2 + 3
1 2 + 3
1 + 2 + 3
1 2 + 3

1 2 3 + 4 +
1 2 3 4 +
1 2 + 3 4 +
1 2 3 + 4 +

1 2 + 3
1 2 3
1 2 3
1 2 3
1 2 + 3
1 2 3
1 2 3
1 2 3

Check Out Your Understanding

In pencil, write the 'count in' and then the counting under the notes below. Remember to add 'shh' underneath any rests too.

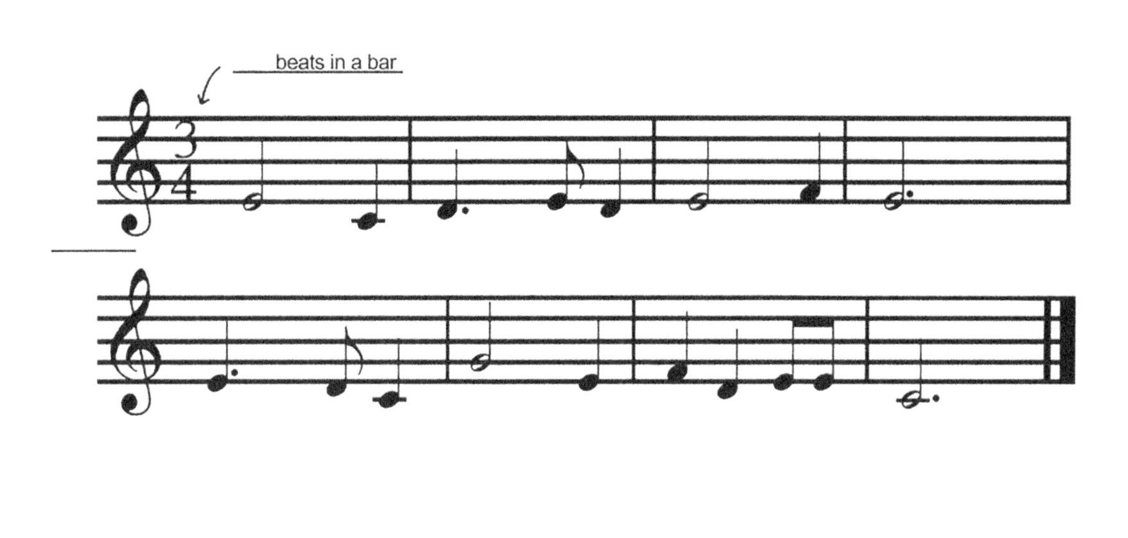

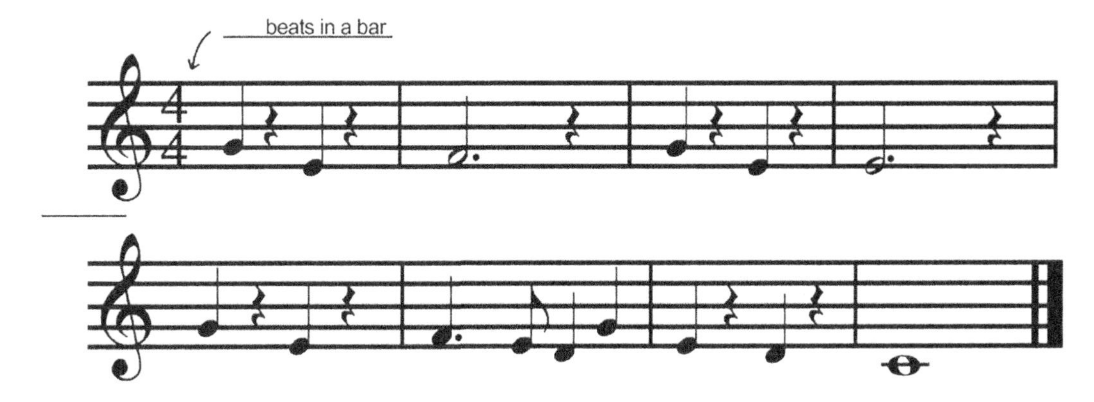

Turn the page and check your answers then count the rhythms of the tunes out loud. →

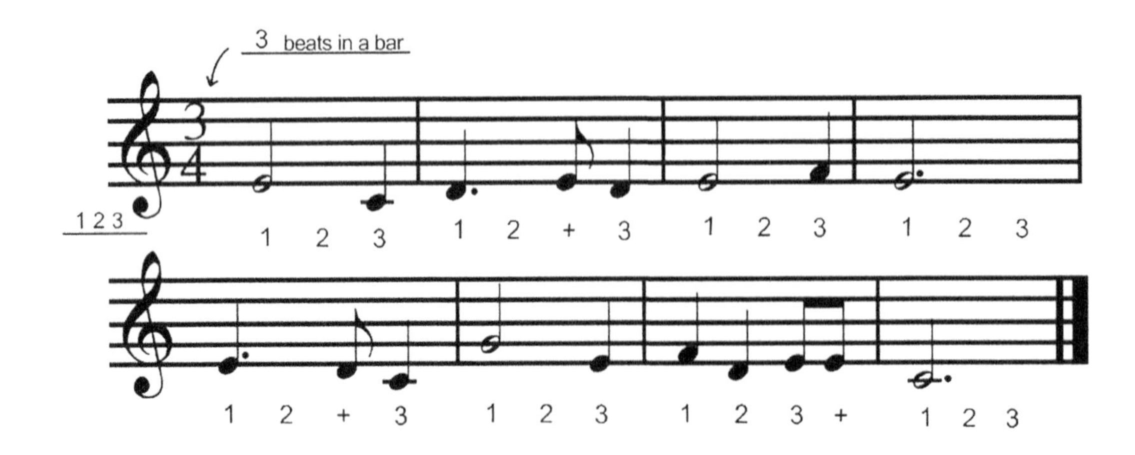
3 beats in a bar
1 2 3
1 2 3 1 2 + 3 1 2 3 1 2 3
1 2 + 3 1 2 3 1 2 3 + 1 2 3

4 beats in a bar
1 2 3 4
1 2 3 4 1 2 3 4 1 2 3 4 1 2 3 4
1 2 3 4 1 2 + 3 4 1 2 3 4 1 2 3 4

CHAPTER 10

PLAY the Next Tunes

- Skills and Knowledge Combine
- The 'Three Step System for Reading Music'
- How to Recognise a Phrase
- Ready to Play? Let's Revise and Exercise

o 'Jingle Bells'
Revise and Exercise: The flow of the first and second time bars, notes 'F' and 'G' and the 'Sound Production Procedure'

o 'Rocking A & Bb'
The key signature of one flat, changing dynamics and throat notes 'A' & 'Bb'

o 'A Minor Creepy Song'
Slurring, notes low 'A' & 'B', 'Associating the Senses' and speed word 'Lento'

o 'Low, Low Down'
Ledger lines, phrasing, note low 'G', playing in the lower part of the instrument

o 'Quavers in G'
The key signature of 'G' Major, playing 'moderato', reading quavers, the Crescendo, the note 'F#'

o 'F Major in 3'
The key signature of 'F' Major, the time signature of ¾, slurring quavers/ eighth notes, the note low 'Bb'

- Scales and Arpeggios Introduced

Skills and Knowledge Combine

The period after the initial lessons is the time you will have the most fun because you will feel comfortable handling the clarinet and produce a reasonably secure sound each time you play. When you add your new literacy skills and understanding of rhythm, learned from the last chapters, you'll be able to interpret many more tunes and widen your repertoire.

The following pages present a series of pieces typical of those you may encounter during the progressive stages of your study. I'm not inferring that you should be able to play one tune after another, because a solid technique and strong sound production must be allowed to evolve and mature over time. The pieces here are merely samples of the level of difficulty that is usually reached, as new notes are gradually introduced in a standard tutor book. Here you will learn how to approach and make sense of them.

Each tune will introduce at least one new note, and a few of the many musical elements that you've already learned, such as key and time signatures, musical signs, symbols and rhythms. Refer to those pages in your tutor book that introduce the same new note as in the tunes here, to supplement your learning.

The underlying objective of this chapter is much more important than the mere understanding and playing of individual tunes – **it is to instill within you a habitual system of reading music** of any kind, which will give you the confidence to read for yourself no matter what the style. Much more importantly, it will bring your playing to life from the start, providing a vehicle through which you can express yourself. Together we will go through the process from seeing the written part to playing the tune and you will be guided all the way.

We have gradually touched on certain principles of reading in previous chapters, so you are used to THINKING the information through, and FEELING and sensing the pulse as you count the rhythms. Here the 'Three Step System for Reading Music' is laid out exactly. Learn these three simple steps from memory and from now on apply them to everything you play:

Three Step System for Reading Music

1. **THINK. Understand all the information** that you are presented with.
2. **FEEL the pulse.** Choose a suitable speed at which to play the music and sense this pulse movement within you before you play.
3. **COUNT yourself in and count as you play.** You THINK the counting to the pulse you FEEL.

How to Recognise a Phrase

A 'phrase' is a small section of music that sounds and feels good on its own. A whole piece of music consists of many phrases put together.

Musicians focus on playing individual phrases with great care. They are 'phrasing' the music. In the beginning stages of learning, you only need to understand this one vital point – the clarinetist plays each phrase with one breath. The column (or sausage) of air pushes through the phrase from the first note to the last, and the air does not stop in the middle. Easy!

Understanding the phrasing of a piece is easy and it will help you to sound even more fabulous as you will breathe in the places that feel the most natural. Without being aware, both the performer and the listener enjoy a piece of music so much more if the breathing – the ins and the out of the breath – flow with the phrasing.

From a very early age, infants breathe in the natural places as they sing nursery rhymes. They have no idea that they are 'phrasing' correctly.

Do this

1. Read the verse of 'Twinkle Twinkle Little Star' aloud. Notice exactly where you take a breath.

    'Twinkle twinkle little star
    How I wonder what you are
    Up above the world so high
    Like a diamond in the sky'

I am sure you will have taken the air in at the end of the lines. The four lines of the poem are perfectly balanced and form four neat phrases.

2. Read the lines again but this time gasp a breath in where the commas are.

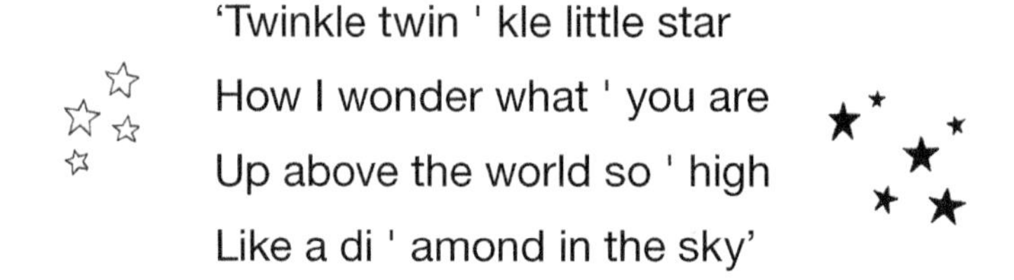

    'Twinkle twin ' kle little star
    How I wonder what ' you are
    Up above the world so ' high
    Like a di ' amond in the sky'

Notice how unnatural and uncomfortable it feels to breathe in the middle of the phrase. You would never do this. You never breathe mid-sentence when speaking either, no matter what the conversation!

3. Sing the words to the tune 'Twinkle Twinkle Little Star'

The phrases of the words fit perfectly into two bar phrases of the music. You will notice that you naturally breathe in at the end of one phrase, to sing the next.

Most of the time musical phrases fit into a regular number of bars and beats. Many songs fall naturally into eight bar phrases whilst some phrases have a natural span of four bars. To keep things simple most phrases in this chapter have a natural length of two bars to enable you to breathe through the total length of the phrase from beginning to end. After a period of learning you will be able to make your breath last through four bars.

You will notice that the phrases start on the first note of the bar and end on the last. At a later stage, you will find phrases that begin and end in different places within the bar. For instance, a phrase may start on the fourth beat of the bar and conclude on the third of another. In these cases, the first and last portion of the phrases invariably add up to make a whole bar. This is not for the immediate concern of the beginner. Working with two bars, starting on the first beat of the bar, is perfect to develop good habitual and natural breathing at this stage.

Phrase markings are not usually present in many music parts, however, composers sometimes support the musician by indicating the phrase with an arch that goes over the top of it. The arched phrase line should not be confused with a slur line which appears much nearer the notes. It is usually left to the performer to be alert to the phrasing and to observe the most natural place to take in the breath. On rare occasions, breath marks, seen as a tick or a comma appear above the stave.

Playing a phrase is just like playing one very long note and moving the fingers around at the same time! Make sure that throughout this chapter and beyond, you play each phrase with one breath and do not break the column of air in the middle of the phrase.

Please note – the counting written underneath the notes and the 'count in' written before the tunes start, are there to support your continued learning. They do not appear in standard music parts.

Special practice requests:

- Practise everything in two bar phrases. Perfect each two bars before you put them all together.
- Practise with your chosen pulse. Do not play the easy bits fast then slow down for the harder bits or the music will not flow and feel good. Play everything slowly at first then increase the speed when you are able.

- 'Count in' every single time, no matter how short the group of notes you are exercising. Play everything to a pulse. Give life and energy to everything you play.

Practising helpful habits from the onset creates a strong foundation on which to build your playing skills and technique!

Ready to Play?

Let's Revise and Exercise! →

'Jingle Bells'

Revise and exercise:

- The flow of the first & second-time bars.
- The notes 'F' and 'G'.
- The 'Sound Production Procedure'.

Step 1 THINK

Observe all the information on the stave.

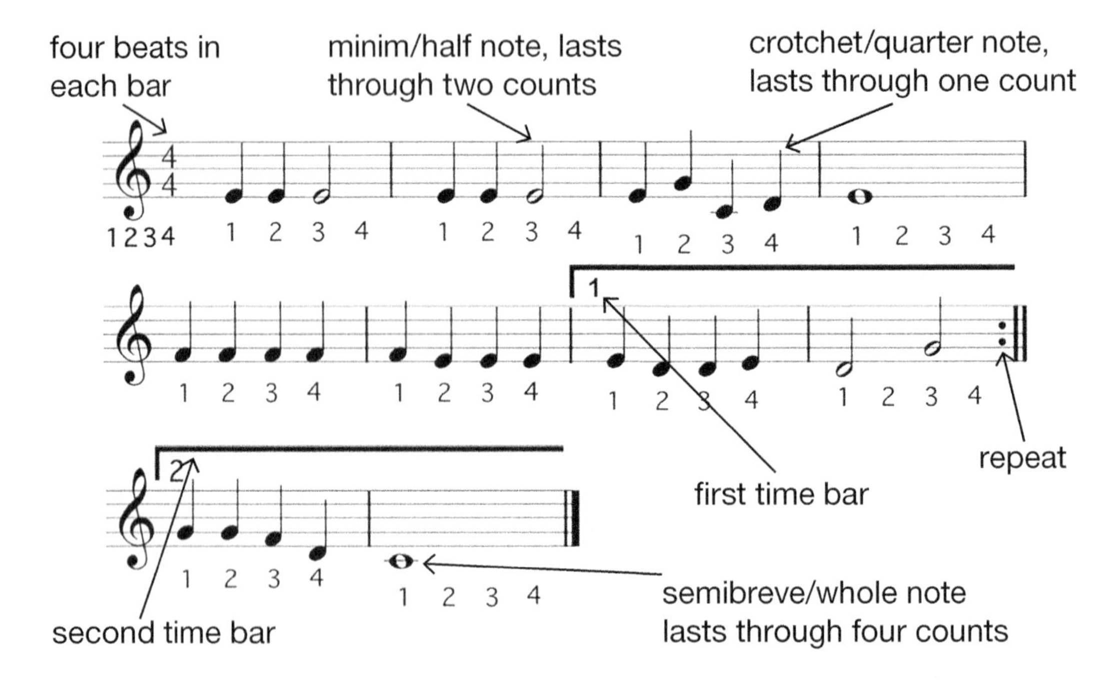

- **The first-time bar** is indicated by a bracket over bars 7 and 8. It is only played the first time through. The repeat at the end of bar 8 goes back to the beginning then at the end of bar 6 jumps to **the second-time bar** to end the tune.
- The tune has five different notes. 'C', 'D', 'E' were introduced in 'PLAY the First Tunes' The new ones here are 'F' and 'G'.
- **The note 'F'** is played with the thumb only.
- **The note 'G'** is played with no fingers or thumb.

Time to play:

- Practise the **'Sound Production Procedure'**:
  1. **Set the embouchure** – rest the reed on the lower overturned lip and anchor the top teeth on the mouthpiece firmly.
  2. **Take the air in** through the **sides of the mouth**.
  3. **Tongue the tip of the reed** to start the note as you push a continuous stream of air firmly through the clarinet.
- Become familiar with the feeling of playing 'F' and 'G' by playing some long notes. If the instrument feels a little unstable as there are no fingers on, pull up slightly with the right-hand thumb, underneath the thumb rest.
- Ensure the sling is at the correct length and that the neckpiece is low down on the neck and taking the weight of the instrument.
- Make the notes even and sweet. Engage with the feeling of the mouth as you play the notes.

Step 2 FEEL the pulse:

- Choose a slow speed to learn the tune and sense this pulse movement inside you.
- It's a good idea to count the rhythm aloud before you play, then you know you've 'got it'.

Step 3 COUNT yourself in and count as you play

You THINK the counting in your head to the pulse you FEEL:

- Learn two bars of 'Jingle Bells' in turn, tonguing every note. Be aware that two bars make a small phrase so last your air column through to the end of each second bar.
- Play the whole tune, breathing in at the end of each two bars only. Imagine you are singing the tune as you play and this will prompt you to last the breath through the phrases.
- Hold the notes through their whole value. The last note of 'Jingle Bells' is held through four counts. Think 'VE – RY – LONG – NOTE'

'Rocking A & Bb'

Revise and exercise:

- The key signature of one flat.
- Changing dynamics.
- The throat notes 'A' and 'Bb'.

Step 1 THINK

Carefully consider all the information on the music stave.

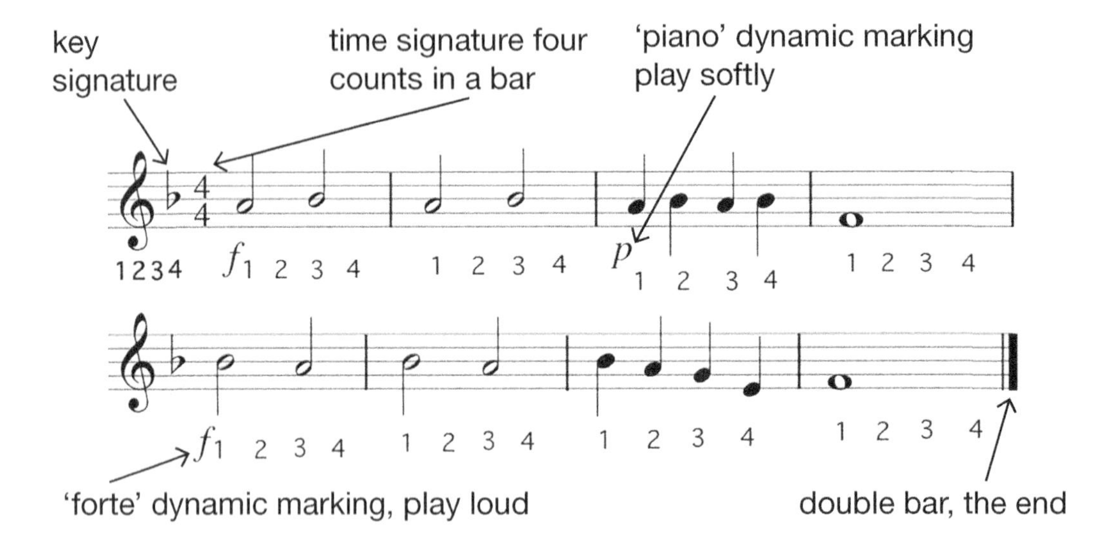

- There is a **key signature of one flat.** The flat sign sits on the middle line where the note 'B' is written. It means play all the 'B' notes as 'Bb'.
- The **dynamics** are written underneath the stave. They change from 'f', meaning play loud, to 'p', meaning play soft. When they change back to loud again in bar five this lasts to the end of the tune.
- **The note 'A'** is played by pressing the tip of the 'A' key with the side of the first finger.

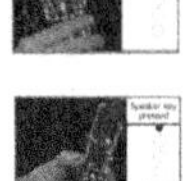

- **The note 'Bb'** is played by pressing the tip of the 'A' key with the side of the first finger and the tip of the speaker key with the tip of the thumb.

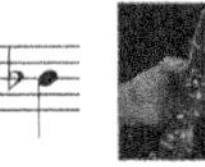

Time to play:

- Twist the wrist! Exercise the first finger of the left hand on the 'A' key. Twist the wrist slightly as you press the *tip* of the key with the side of the first finger. Rock on and off playing 'A', 'G', 'A', 'G', until the movement becomes fluent and smooth.
- Exercise the fingering of 'Bb'. Press the 'A' key, then the tip of the speaker key, with the tip of the thumb. Pivot the thumb slightly at the knuckle and keep it clear of the thumb hole as you play 'A', 'Bb', 'A', 'Bb' repeatedly, until the action of the thumb becomes smooth.

Step 2 FEEL the pulse:

- Set the pulse to a slow beat. Only increase the pulse when you have learned the tune. Sense this pulse movement inside you.
- Count yourself in and point to the numbers underneath the stave, with your finger or a pencil, as you confidently count out loud.

Step 3 COUNT yourself in and count as you play:

You THINK the counting to the pulse you FEEL:

- Play the first two bars of 'Rocking A & Bb' 'forte' – loudly. Hold this dynamic throughout. Keep the tone even, making sure you do not overblow and distort the sound.
- Play the next two bars 'piano' – softly. Make a clear sound.
- Play the last four bars 'forte'. Can you last the breath through the four bars to make a four-bar phrase? If not, that is not a problem. Take a breath at the end of the second bar. You will be able to last the air column over four bars in time.

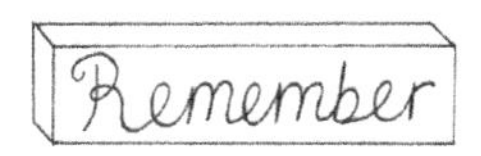

- Keep the left thumb clear of the thumb hole when it is not needed for 'A' and 'Bb'. Never rest the thumb on the body of the clarinet.
- Keep the side of the first fingers away from the side keys to avoid squeaks.

'A Minor Creepy Song'

Revise and exercise:

- Slurring.
- The notes low 'B' and 'A'.
- 'Associating the Senses' – see, hear and feel the notes.
- The speed indication 'Lento'.

Step 1 THINK

Take in everything on the stave that you read.

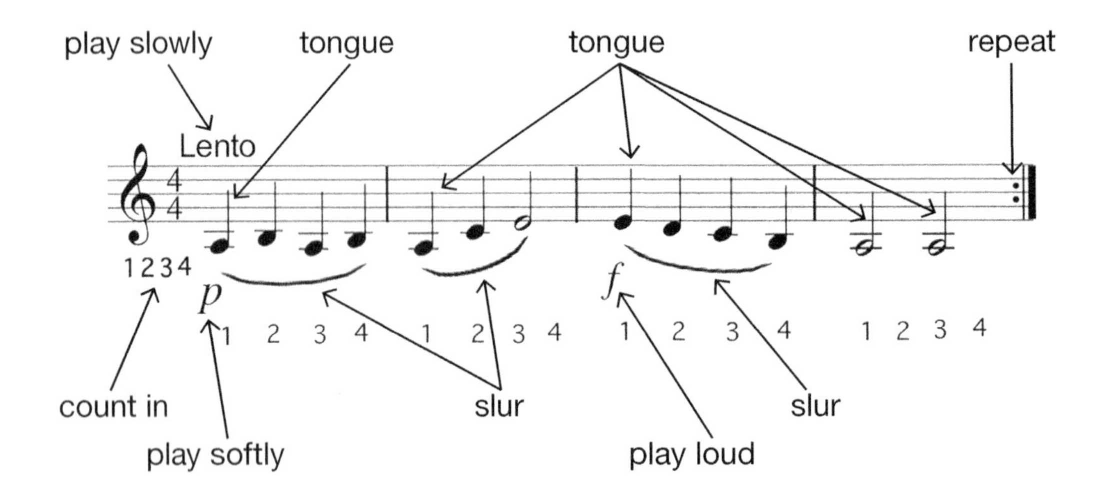

- **Slur lines** join the notes inside the first three bars.
- There is a **repeat sign** at the end of the last bar.
- There are **dynamic marks** giving contrast between soft and loud sections.
- **Low 'B'** is played with the thumb and the first three fingers of the left hand, at the top of the clarinet, and the second finger of the right hand at the bottom.

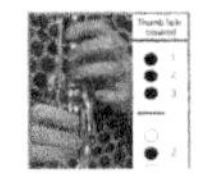

- **Low 'A'** is played with the thumb, the top three fingers of the left hand and the top two fingers of the right hand.

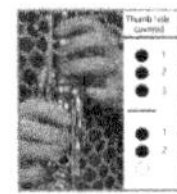

Time to play:

- **'Associate the Senses'** as you play long notes low 'B' and 'A':

  LISTEN to the sound.

  FEEL the fingers on the clarinet and sense the mouth position.

  LOOK at the note position on the stave.

Linking the senses of sound, touch and sight makes learning a meaningful, deeper experience than merely 'thinking' the fingering for the note.

As you play the long notes, appreciate the distance the air travels down the instrument. Push the air constantly with some speed, imagining it reaches the very bottom of the clarinet.

- **Remember the rules about slurring** – when a note is not joined to a previous note by a slur line, it is tongued. When a note is joined to a previous note by a slur line, it is slurred not tongued.
- **Exercise slurring.** Tongue the note 'E' then put one finger down at a time without tonguing – 'E' 'D' 'C' 'B' 'A' and hold the last note on as long as you can. You have slurred the notes 'E' to low 'A'.

Step 2 FEEL the pulse:

- **The speed indication 'Lento'**, at the top left of the piece means 'slowly'. Stand up and march slowly on the spot and feel the regular movement of slow steps within your body. You have 'set the pulse'. Keep this slow and regular sense of movement within you throughout your practice.

Step 3 COUNT yourself in and count as you play:

Work a bar at a time for the first three bars:

- Tongue the first note then slur the rest.
- Push the air *through* the clarinet. Push the air *through* the bar.
- Exaggerate the loud phrases after the soft ones to shock the listener. This is, after all, 'A Minor *Creepy* Song'!

'Low Low Down'

Revise and exercise:

- Ledger lines.
- Spotting the phrases and breathing with them.
- The note low 'G'.
- Playing in the lower part of the instrument.

Step 1 THINK

What can you read in this part?

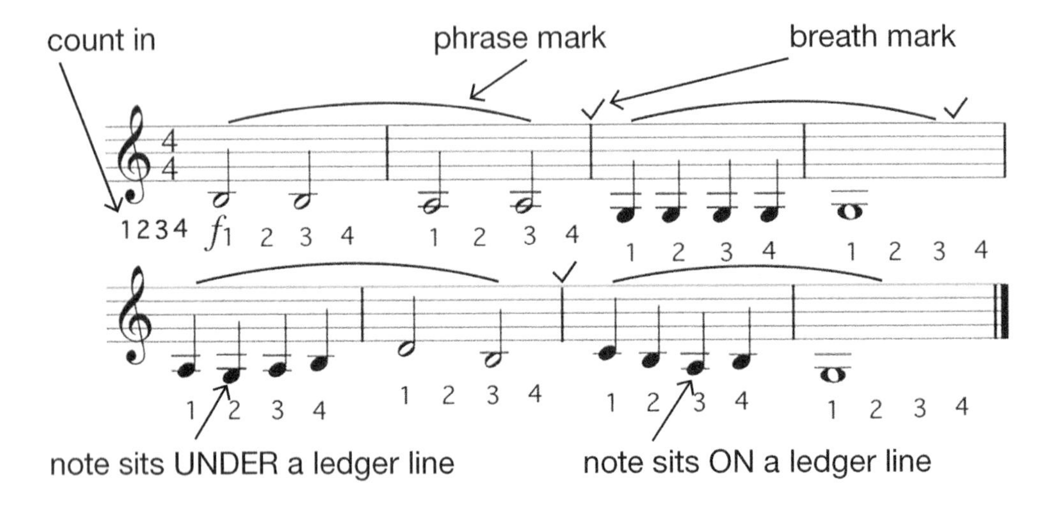

- Notes written below the stave sit either ON or BELOW small lines called **'ledger lines'**.
- **The phrase markings** are the lines that go over two bars. They draw your attention to the small units and encourage you to play each phrase with one breath. In many cases phrase markings are not written in music parts.
- **The breath marks** are like small ticks. They remind you to breathe at the ends of the phrases and not in the middle.
- **The four-beat 'count in'** before the piece starts prompts you to count yourself in before everything you play so all your music sits with the pulse.
- **Low 'G' i**s played with the thumb and first three fingers of the left hand and the first three fingers of the right hand.

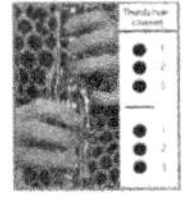

Time to play:

- **Feel comfortable playing at the bottom of the instrument**. If these notes are a challenge remember the **Low Note Tips** – play them with:
  1. **Firm Fingers** – Make sure the holes are covered completely by the pads of the fingers, and that the ring keys are fully pressed.
  2. **Firm Air** – Play with a strong column of air imagining it is travelling right through down to the bell of the clarinet.
  3. **Firm Tongue** – Articulate the reed lightly but purposefully with the tip of the tongue.
- When a low note seems to refuse to come out, play down to it from a higher note that you can play easily. Tongue the note 'C' (three fingers) then slur down to 'G' putting one finger down at a time. 'C', 'B', 'A', 'G'. Hold the 'G' at the end and as you HEAR the sound LOOK at the symbol of the sound as it is written. At the same time put your attention on how the fingers and the mouth FEEL as the note is achieved. You will be surprised how your brain will remember the minute physical feeling of the mouth position as it plays a note, and how quickly you will reproduce notes after a short time.

Step 2 FEEL the pulse:

- Choose your speed wisely. Always sense a speed at which you can play the whole tune. Never start a tune quickly because it is easy, then after a couple of bars slow it down because you can't play the notes. In the case of 'Low Low Down', play with a slow pulse so you have plenty of time to exercise 'firm fingers, firm air, firm tongue'.

Step 3 COUNT yourself in and count as you play:

- Exercise each two-bar phrase individually, counting the movement of the notes with the pulse and tonguing all the way! Remember to 'count in' *everything* you practise.
- Push the air through the phrase and make it last to the very end. There you will notice the breath mark and it will feel natural to breathe in, ready to play the next phrase – just as if you were reading one line of a poem aloud, then breathing in to read the next line.

'Quavers in G'

Revise and exercise:

• The key signature of 'G' Major • Playing 'moderato' • Reading quavers/ eighth notes • The crescendo • The note 'F#'.

Step 1 THINK

What are the symbols in this piece that are less familiar to you?

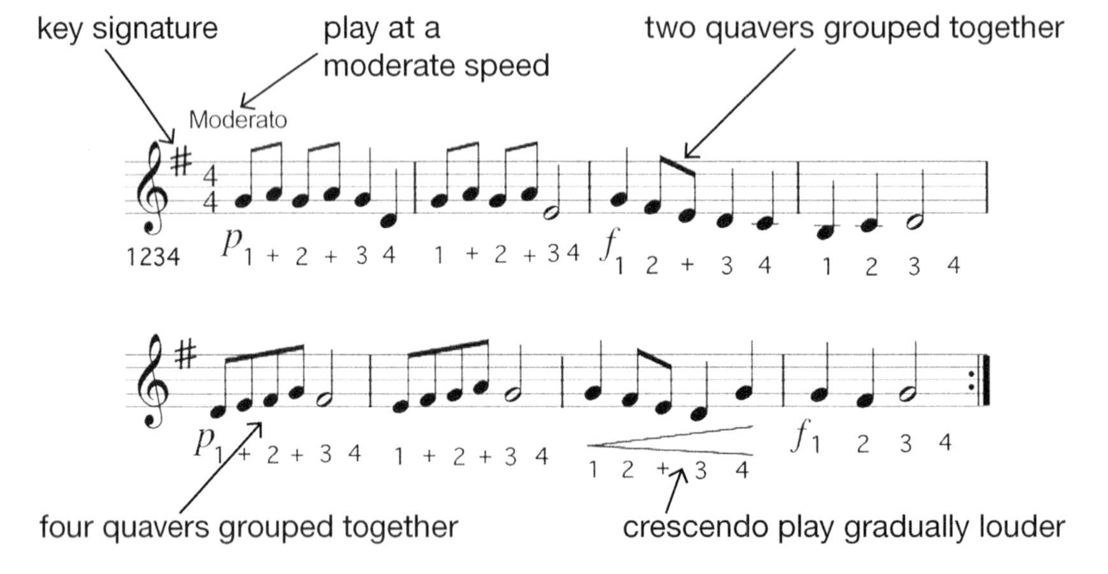

- **The key signature** has one sharp which sits ON the 'F' line meaning play all the 'F' notes in the piece as 'F#'. The piece is in the **key of 'G' major.** 'G' major has a key signature of one sharp and that is always 'F#'. Run your finger underneath the stave and count all the 'F' notes that have been affected by the sharp sign (#) sitting on the 'F' line. I can count six.
- **The speed word 'moderato'** means play at a moderate speed.
- **The half-beat quavers** are grouped in 2's and 4's. Each second, off-beat quaver is counted as 'and'.
- **The 'crescendo'** mark in bar 7 increases the volume. This bar starts softly and builds throughout to reach 'forte' in the last bar.
- **The note 'F#'** is played with the first finger of the left hand (no thumb).  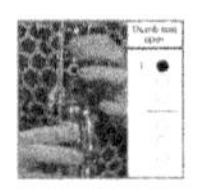

Time to play:

- **Be stable with 'F#'. If the clarinet feels wobbly** as there is only one finger down:
    1. Pull it upwards very slightly with the right-hand thumb under the thumb rest.
    2. Give the weight of the instrument to the neckpiece of the sling.
- Exercise lots of long 'F#' notes using the tips above and notice how you gradually feel more comfortable with the stability of the instrument.

Tip – keep the left thumb clear of the thumb hole but not too far away from it and never be tempted to put it on the clarinet to aid with stability.

Step 2 FEEL the pulse:

- Set a moderate pulse for this tune. Count the rhythm aloud before you play to revise the feeling of the quaver rhythms fitting into the space of the beat '1&, 2&' etc.

Step 3 COUNT yourself in and count as you play:

- Pause to think what this step means! It is a rule for everything you play. *Count in before everything* – even when you are working on a single bar!
- Follow the principle of making the air last through each two-bar phrase. Make this a good habit from now on.
- Give attention to the crescendo bar pushing more air gradually through the bar. Make the increasing volume even and smooth.

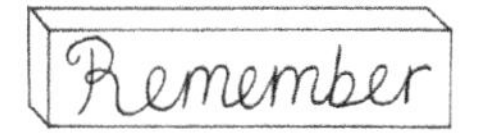

Every so often, give some attention to check your:

- Posture – A straight back allows you to breathe well.
- Clarinet angle – An angle of about 40° away from the body allows the air to pass through the mouthpiece.
- Length of the sling – Make sure it's perfect so you don't strain your neck.
- Music stand distance and height – Keep at a height so you don't move the neck either up or down and at a suitable distance so you can hold your clarinet out well.

'F Major in 3'

Revise and exercise:

• The key signature of 'F' Major • Playing with the time signature of ¾ • Slurring quavers/eighth notes • The note low 'Bb'.

Step 1 THINK

Take time to interpret, understand and work out the 'geography' of the piece.

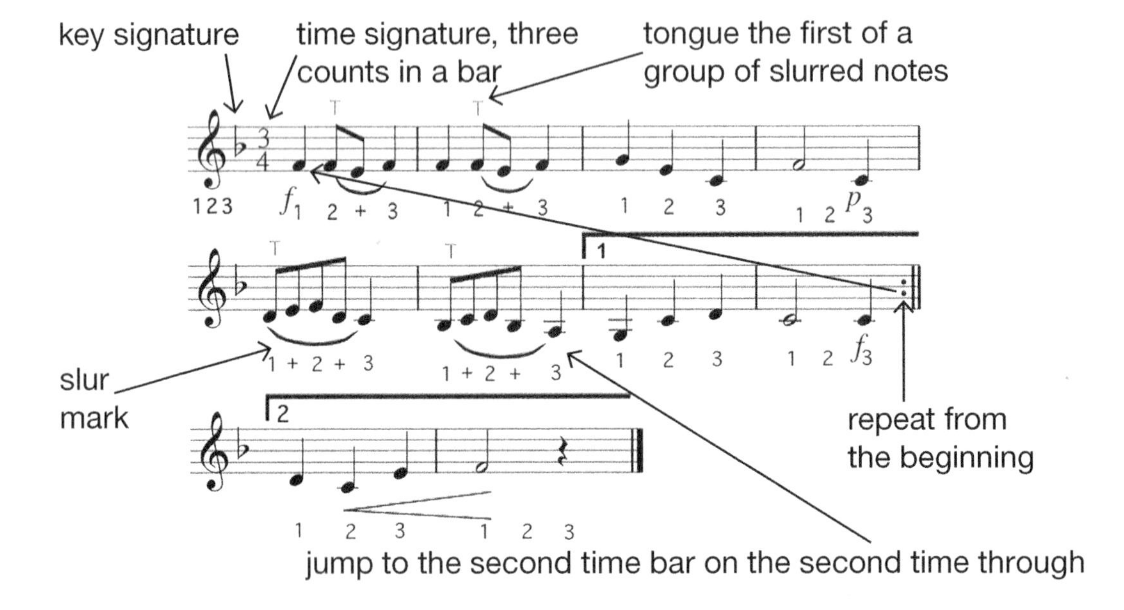

- **The key signature** has one flat sitting ON the middle line flattening all the notes named 'B'. The piece is in the **key of 'F' major**. 'F' major has a key signature of one flat which is always 'Bb'. Notice the key signature appears at the beginning of each line. Cast your eye through to see if there are any 'B' notes that are affected by the key signature – see bar 6.
- **The time signature** is ¾ meaning there are three beats in each bar and the value of those beats is a crotchet.
- **The slurred groups of quavers** all have a 'T' above the first note to remind you to tongue the first note and slur the rest of the group.
- **The 'geography'** of the piece is: at the end of bar 8 repeat back to the beginning and on the second time through jump from the end of bar 6 to the second-time bar.

- **Note low 'Bb'** is played with the thumb and first three fingers of the left hand and on the lower joint, the first finger of the right hand covers the first hole.

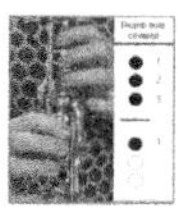

Time to play:

- **Make the best quality low 'Bb' note** you can. Listen carefully as you play your long note exercises and ask yourself **Sensible Sound Questions**:
  1. Is my sound sweet and pure or do I sound harsh?
  2. Is my sound even? Am I pushing an even column of air through the clarinet or a wobbly one?
  3. Is my sound keeping the same in pitch or is it going higher (sharper) or lower (flatter) at the ends?
- Link up the senses as you fully 'experience' the note. LOOK and observe the appearance of the Bb sitting underneath one ledger line and HEAR the tone quality of the note and FEEL the fingers as you cover the holes and experience the sensation of the air travelling down the clarinet.

Step 2 FEEL the pulse:

- Set a slow pulse for this tune. Appreciate that you are less familiar with three beats in a bar so take time to experience the feeling of the ¾ pulse. Emphasise the number '**1**' as you sense '**1**, 2, 3, **1**, 2, 3, **1**, 2, 3, **1**, 2, 3'.
- Point to the helpful counting underneath the notes as you count aloud and establish the rhythm before you play.

Step 3 COUNT yourself in and count as you play:

- Work at bars 1 and 2 giving attention to the correct tonguing and slurring then the same with bars 5 and 6. Make sure that you play 'Bb's in bar 6.
- Play each two bars in turn lasting the air through the smooth phrase.
- Be dynamic with the dynamics – exaggerate the contrast between the loud and soft sections for an exciting effect.

Scales and Arpeggios Introduced

Scales and arpeggios are vitally important. The patterns of notes within them form the foundation of our technique.

A scale is a pattern of notes going from one note to the same named note an octave above. Just as an octopus has eight legs an octave has eight notes.

Scales have names. The name of this **scale is 'F' Major.** It has a key signature of one flat. The single flat sign sits on the line on which the note 'B' is written, telling us to now play all the 'B' notes as 'Bb'.

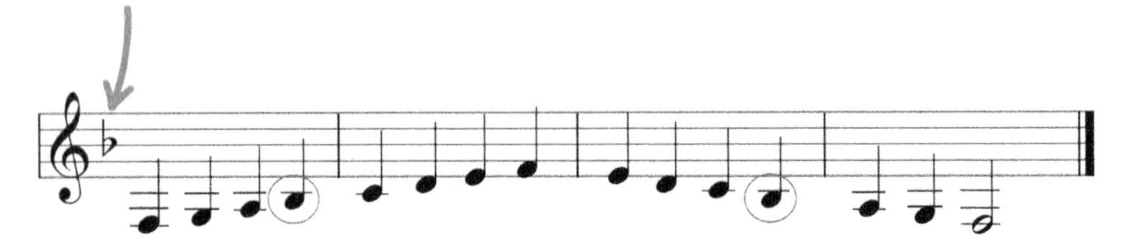

An arpeggio is made up of the first, the third and the fifth note of the scale. Instruments that can play more than one note at a time such as pianos and guitars, sometimes play these notes together forming what is called a 'chord'. As single note instrumentalists, we practise our arpeggio patterns up and down one note at a time.

Here you can see that the **arpeggio of 'F' major** is made up of the 'F', the first note of the scale, 'A', the third note of the scale and 'C', the fifth note of the scale and then of course, the octave note.

This is the **scale of 'G' Major.** 'G' Major has one sharp in the key signature. This sharp sign sits on the top line of the stave which is the line on which the note 'F' is written. The sharp sign on this line tells us to play all the 'F' notes as 'F#'.

Here is the **arpeggio of 'G' Major**. Notice that it is made up of 'G', the first note of the scale, 'B', the third note and 'D', the fifth of the scale.

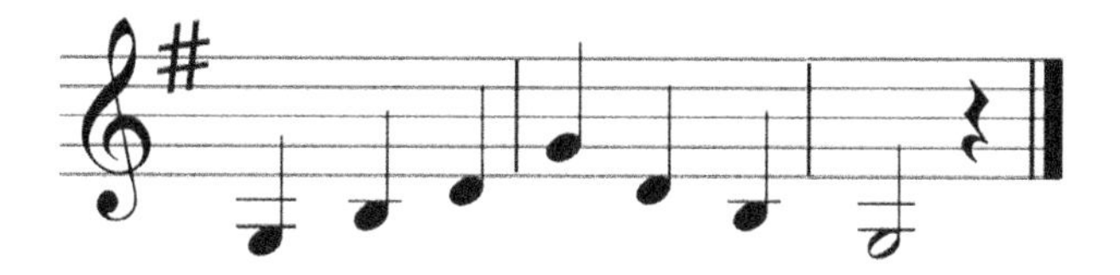

Practise scales and arpeggios rhythmically with the pulse.

There is no point in playing the series of notes without having any feeling for the pulse. These note patterns appear repeatedly in pieces of music. If you fit the notes with the pulse from the onset you will reproduce them in that way in the future. You will play them 'rhythmically'.

- To practise a scale play to a pulse of 4 in a bar.
- To practise an arpeggio, play to a pulse of 3 in a bar.

Notice the difference between the pattern of the notes in the scale and the pattern of the notes in the arpeggio above.

- The eight notes of the scale fit neatly into two bars with four beats in each. When you practise the scale, count 4 beats in and then play counting '1, 2, 3, 4, 1, 2, 3, 4' and make the first note of the bar heavier and accented.
- The three notes of the arpeggio fit neatly into one bar. Set the pulse and count 3 beats in, then count '1, 2, 3, 1, 2, 3', again, making the first note of the bar heavier and accented.

CHAPTER 11

Whoops! Got a Problem?

- Sound Not Coming Out?
- Clarinet Leaking?
- Are You Squeaking?
- Got a Watery Sound?
- Water in the Tone Holes?
- Got a Sore Thumb?
- Clarinet Wobbling in Your Mouth?
- Not Sounding Right?

The path to getting to grips with the clarinet can be quite an adventure! As on any long journey, there will be a variety of surprises. As well as having a smooth ride, there'll be a few hills to climb, diversions in the road, and, here and there the odd ditch to get you off track. Even if you stay in the same place playing the same tunes and exercises for a while, you'll have great satisfaction as you eventually turn the corner, realise you, 'get it' and that playing this instrument is not only well within your reach but huge fun into the bargain!

If you want enjoyment all the way, simply accept any snags that interrupt the flow! They're just part of the natural learning process. Instead of labeling a situation as a 'problem' see it as a challenge. Don't fall into the trap of feeling despondent when you're stuck, and give up in disappointment. Locate the answer straight away, and you'll be back on track in no time.

Here are the most common challenges that some beginners experience, along with some helpful suggestions how to deal with them.

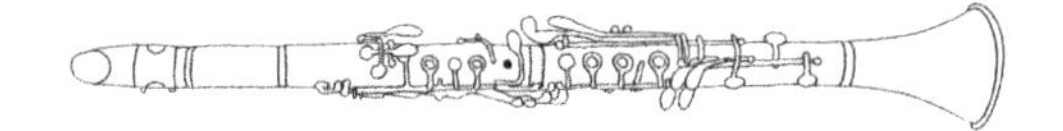

Sound Not Coming Out?

Make sure:

- **The reed is a suitable strength.**

  Use number 1½ at the beginning. Harder reeds are harder to play. You can move on to a number 2 reed once you have been playing for a while and have built up some strength in the embouchure.

- **You have the right amount of mouthpiece in your mouth.**

  If you are playing with just the tip of the mouthpiece in the mouth, the reed will partially close to the mouthpiece preventing it vibrating well. With too much mouthpiece in the mouth, the sound may not happen either (or you may squeak). Have a good look at the mouthpiece from the side. Notice the place where the mouthpiece leaves the reed. Rest the reed on the lower lip at this point. The top teeth then come down to the top of the mouthpiece in the corresponding place, keeping the gap open and allowing the reed to vibrate to its potential.

  It may be easy to understand this, but it can be difficult for a beginner to feel the best distance of the mouthpiece in the mouth. The action of slowly pushing the tip of the mouthpiece into the mouth as you slowly push air into the instrument will ensure you feel the exact place where the sound engages. Refer to the 'Quick Sound Instruction' exercise in Chapter 3 for extra help with this.

- **You are not biting the mouthpiece and closing the gap so that the air won't go through.**

  Recognize that all biting action comes from the lower jaw moving upwards towards the top jaw. Even if you feel you are producing the sound successfully it is worth having a look at the top of the mouthpiece every so often. A tell-tale sign that you are biting, is the appearance of teeth marks on the beak. Beginners think it's the top teeth that have created these marks but it is the bottom jaw biting upwards. Bearing this in mind, release the lower jaw downwards bringing the reed away from the mouthpiece and increasing the gap for the air to get through. Think 'jaw to floor' while keeping the lower lip cushioning the reed, stretched to the sides a little and, of course, maintaining the slight 'smile' at the mouth corners.

Always take conscious steps never to grip or bite the mouthpiece.

Clarinet Leaking?

If there are any leaks from the holes under the key work, you have no chance of creating the sound evenly. When a clarinet is not working, it is not a disaster, it just needs fixing.

If your clarinet is new from the shop, you can expect it in tip top condition. The mechanism is intricate and interlinking, so it's imperative that it is working smoothly. You should not have to press the keys ridiculously hard.

When instruments arrive from abroad, they are often 'corked,' meaning that certain parts of the mechanism are kept in place by the insertion of small pieces of cork to prevent any movement during the shipping. A vigilant distributor will ensure that every instrument is examined and adjusted before sale. Occasionally one may slip through the net, so if your clarinet is leaking or the key work is stiff or jammed take it back to the shop at once and explain. Most stores are happy to sort it out on the spot, and you should not expect to pay for any adjustments made.

To detect leaks from the key work.

Check the middle joints in turn. Make sure that the tops of these joints are scrupulously clean.

Top joint:

- Cover the three top holes and the thumb hole with the left-hand fingers.
- Press the bottom of the top joint on to the flat part of the right hand.
- Put the lips on the top of the joint. You have now made a complete seal around all the apertures so no air should enter or exit from any of the key holes.

- Try to blow air into the joint and then make a sucking motion. Repeat. It will be obvious if any air is leaking in or out. Listen for it hissing out and get someone to put a hand around the joint to feel for any escaping air and if so which hole is it escaping from.

Bottom joint:

- Seal the three holes with the right-hand first fingers.
- Press the fourth finger on the low 'E' Key – this is the bottom key on the furthest right, of the four keys, which closes the lowest hole below it.
- Press the bottom of the joint into the flat part of the left hand.
- Put the lips on to the top of the joint.
- Blow, suck, blow, suck as before to see if any of the holes are leaking.

If you have some leaks, then it’s time to have the clarinet serviced. My preference is always to seek a professional repairer who will replace or adjust the pads and ensure they are 'seating' correctly on the holes. There are invariably a few extra mechanical adjustments necessary. It's always refreshing to get your instrument back playing smoother than before.

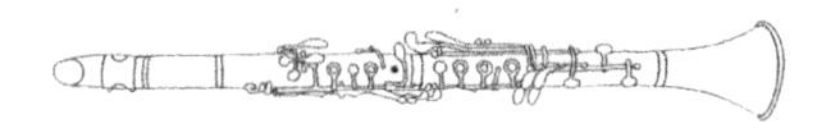

Are You Squeaking?

There are lots of reasons why squeaks happen. Sometimes they're difficult to pinpoint so explore all these ideas. If air jumps randomly out of a hole that it shouldn't, you will create a prize squeak! Like a mouse jumping out of a hole, it's always unexpected. It always takes you by surprise! **To find where the squeak is coming from, consider both the open holes** covered by the fingers **and the holes under the key work** with pads, which you may mistakenly open with the sides of the fingers. Check out all the following points – otherwise, you may have a family of mice taking nest in your clarinet!

Check out the fingers and hands – make sure that:

- **The fleshy part of the fingers and thumb are covering the open finger holes completely.** If you're not sure, press them firmly down on to the holes with a lot of pressure. If you can then see the impression of a full circle on the finger ends you know that you are fully covering those holes and that no air can be leaking from them. If you can't, it may mean that your fingers are going too far over the holes and allowing air to escape.

- **You are pressing the ring keys** that go around the finger holes entirely.

- **The thumb is not touching the tip of the speaker** key at the back, by mistake.

- **The sides of the first fingers are not touching the side keys.** Do not be tempted to help support the weight of the clarinet by hooking the right first finger underneath the side key. Keep the finger completely away from this key for now. You will find that your left-hand first finger is directly above a key. These side keys are two of the main offenders for causing squeaks. As you can't see the fingers when you play, you need to be aware of the feeling in the hands. If you maintain a natural 'C' shape in both hands, between the thumb and the first finger, it should be easy to keep clear of these keys. Having the middle fingers at right-angles to the clarinet also helps.

Check out the mouth position – make sure that:

- **The mouthpiece is not too far in the mouth.** Remember that the reed rests on the bottom lip at the place where the mouthpiece leaves the reed. Try pulling it out a bit if you are not sure.

- **The lower teeth are not touching the reed.**

- **The clarinet is not held out too high.** Try to keep the angle of the instrument about 40° from the body.

- **Air is not leaking** from the sides of the mouth as you play.

- **You are not biting** and closing the gap between the reed and the mouthpiece.
- **You are remembering to tongue** and not trying to start the note by pushing the air through randomly.
- **You are not forcing the air** through harshly.

Check out the reed is:

- **In good condition**, not split, chipped, or just worn out. You will recognise the latter as you become more experienced as it will not be totally responsive to playing.
- **Set correctly** on the mouthpiece, and the ligature is not nipping it.

Got a Watery Sound?

Clearing the excess moisture from both the front and back of the reed makes an instant difference to the clarity of the sound.

It's easy to hear if there is a lot of water on the reed as the sound will not be clear but beginners tend not to be alert to this at first. It's rather like a sizzling sound so listen out.

To clear the water from the front of the reed:

- Press the flat thumb firmly from the base of the reed up and over the tip. Do this once only. You will not damage the tip of the reed going from base to tip. Do not rub the reed up and down with your thumb.

To take the water from the back of the reed:

- Suck the mouthpiece once quickly!

When you are accustomed to clearing the reed of water the procedure can be done in the shortest time, in the space of a few beats rest, making an immediate difference to the clarity of the sound.

Water in the Tone Holes?

You will soon start to recognise when water has trickled into a hole that is covered by a pad. When a gurgling sound masks a good note, it can be frustrating – especially if you happen to be playing a solo at the time. As the natural condensation from the breath runs through the clarinet, it finds a trail and sticks to it. Sometimes the trail goes through a tone hole.

Manage waterlogged holes:

- **Be aware of any holes that tend to get waterlogged** and keep an eye on them. They are different on various clarinets.

- **Keep using the pull-through** during playing sessions to dry the trickle of water.

- **Blow the water out of the hole**. Press the key to open a waterlogged hole then blow across it to remove most of the water.

- **Use absorbent paper underneath the pad to absorb the excess water.** You may be able to purchase this from the same shop as you bought the clarinet. The old fashioned and the much cheaper way is to use cigarette paper. Put the paper underneath the pad. Gently press the top of the key down on the paper to absorb the moisture. Move the paper so a dry piece is under the pad and press again. Repeat till all the moisture is absorbed.

- **Oil the bore of the clarinet.** Only use the kind sold for this purpose. Put sparingly onto a 'pull-through' cloth, and pass this through the dry bore of the clarinet a few times. Sometimes this can change the flow of the water thus avoiding clogging the problematic hole.

Got a Sore Thumb?

In the beginning, your right-hand thumb may suffer a little. If you're keeping it straight and supporting the thumb rest between the nail and knuckle, well done. The only problem is that your thumb may get a bit sore in this position until you get used to playing.

Before the thumb has gained much strength, you may find your hand has crept around a little, and you are supporting the thumb rest in the crook of the hand. This position is unhelpful as it doesn't allow the fingers to operate on the holes correctly. Persevere putting the thumb rest between the nail and the knuckle and you will strengthen the thumb in time.

To help a sore thumb:

- **Use the sling.** Take all the weight of the clarinet on the neckpiece of the sling and off the thumb. Use the thumb merely to guide the clarinet into the playing position. Your thumb will feel relieved. For comfort and ease, ensure the neckpiece is as low down on the neck as possible, and over the clothing. Make sure the sling is at a length which enables the mouthpiece to go into the mouth without moving the neck either forward or backward – otherwise your neck will ache! If you use a sling, take extra care to push the clarinet away from you to play. Do not allow it to hang down near your body.

- **Use a rubber rest** which fits tightly over the thumb rest if you don't have a ring on the thumb rest to take a sling. Once in place, it will give great comfort to the thumb.

- **Have a piece of felt or cork under the rest,** so your thumb is not in contact with bare metal.

Clarinet Wobbling in Your Mouth?

If the instrument is wobbling in your mouth, it means that you are playing it in your lips. That's not a good idea, so try out the following:

- **Make sure the top teeth are down on top of the mouthpiece securely.** This does not imply biting in any way – it means anchoring the teeth to the mouthpiece. If you **use a mouthpiece patch stuck to the top side of the mouthpiece**, your top teeth will feel more comfortable. I recommend this to all my students. The thick black patches have a spongier feel than the see through, thinner ones.

- **Keep your head in a neutral position. Imagine you are putting the whole weight of the head down a fraction** and sense the teeth firmly on the top of the mouthpiece. Just imagine that you are very slightly putting the whole head down a fraction.

- **Slightly pull up with the thumbs** to adhere the top teeth to the mouthpiece.

- **Stretch the sides of the mouth** a little as if you were grinning. Keep the mouthpiece stable between the top teeth and the bottom lip, while the lips part to take in air.

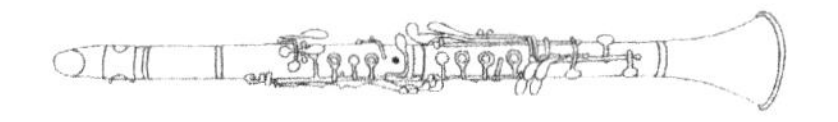

Not Sounding Right?

Sometimes you may feel you have got everything right – you have assembled the clarinet well, your mouth is in a perfect position, you are playing the right notes, articulating well and counting the rhythms – yet the playing just doesn't seem to feel right, and it's not engaging!

Bring on The Two Golden Rules!

The even pulse and the controlled air column are the recipe for making any piece of music hot and exciting. See these golden rules as your golden tools that you can implement to bring your music alive – every time, in every style, in every place!

If your playing is not sounding right, given that all the technical factors are in place...

Reflect on the pulse – ask yourself:

- 'Am I setting the pulse and sensing it within me before I play?'
- 'Am I counting myself in, in my head – before I play?'
- 'Am I counting to this inner pulse as I play?'

Reflect on the air column – ask yourself:

- 'Am I pushing an even controlled column of air through the instrument?'
- 'Is the air column lasting for the whole phrase, right to the end?'
- 'Am I rounding off the end of the phrase then breathing in, to prepare for the next phrase?'

Want to stand out from the crowd?
Play with the pulse and control the air through each phrase!
Hot stuff!

CHAPTER 12

Practice is Magic

- Practice is Magic
- How Long Should I Practise?
- Become a Musical Athlete!
- The ‘Lip’
- Don’t Want to Play?
- What Exactly to Practise?
- The 'Daily Practice Plan for All Round Development’
- Practical How to Practise Tips
- The ‘Practising Checklist for Beginners’
- Amazing Attitude! Bring it on!
- On a Final Note – Access your FREE online course ‘Clarinet Kickstart’
- Wishing You Every Success

Practice is Magic

There is no doubt about it, when you practise regularly, in a happy mood and with good energy, magical transformations can take place with your playing. Beautiful creations come out your instrument which is only a tube with holes, keys, and a reed. The music is, of course, coming from inside you. You develop your technique then use the instrument as a vehicle for expressing your musicianship.

One certainty about practising is that it simply must be done – there is no getting away from it! Whether you are aiming for a professional career or simply playing for fun, practice is necessary to either maintain or develop a standard of playing.

All the musicians you see in a professional setting – the television, at a rock concert, the opera or in a folk group, etc. – they have all practised and prepared for their performance. Always aspire to the standard of great players. Although you may feel in awe, you must refuse to believe, even for one moment, that you could never reach a high level of playing. Take great comfort in remembering that every player you admire was once a beginner too, learning the process of playing the instrument, how to handle it and manage it, how to listen and produce the beautiful tone, how to engage their playing with the natural rhythm and flow within them, and how to interpret the written parts. All this had to be studied, and all players go through similar steps to mastering the instrument. Without a doubt, professional clarinetists over the years have made the same mistakes and had very similar challenges to those you may be experiencing.

Of course, some musicians may have more of a natural flair than others, but in most cases, it is the amount of practising that has taken place which makes the difference between a fantastic player and an average one.

Now, I by no means recommend that you make yourself a slave to practising – I suggest the very opposite! I want you to know that whatever level or standard you aspire to – you can get there. Bring on the enthusiasm, determination and the will to succeed and who knows?!

How Long Should I Practise?

If you're considering the length of your practice time, dump the word 'should' – don't even go there! Thinking about it in this way invariably leads to a negative feeling of either obligation to practise, if you don't want to, or a sense of guilt that you haven't practised when you 'should' have. Asking 'How long 'could' I practise?' leaves you feeling so much more upbeat and raring to go. Since this music business is all about pleasure and nothing else – or at least it could be, for both the performer and the listener – stay on the side of enjoying every single note you play!

An obvious and huge consideration is that practising creates habits. Doing something repeatedly invariably enables us to do it automatically without thinking. Just as with everything else, in playing there are those habits that are helpful to us and those that are not. The truth is that the **better practising habits get us what we want** – a beautiful sound, fluency and ease of playing and ability to communicate to the listener with musical and sensory playing. On the other hand, the **unhelpful habits**, of course, **get us what we don't want** – insecure playing, a weak tone and an arhythmical style of playing which no one will listen to. It goes without saying – the way of the practice can either expand or diminish a player's enthusiasm.

The beginner's first learning is mostly about handling the instrument well and with ease, and of course making the lovely sound. You will appreciate that there are so many important small things to put together at once to play successfully. I hope you will agree that they are all relatively easy to understand and apply – yet omitting any one of them can prevent you playing as well as you could. For instance, if you forgot to set the reed on the mouthpiece correctly, you would struggle to make a good sound, and if you breathe in through your nose instead of the sides of your mouth, it would be so difficult to play. You would be in despair in no time.

I strongly recommend that you keep referring to the 'Practising Checklist' at the end of this chapter each time you exercise. It is a succinct summary of the most important tips that will keep you on track and get you playing with speed and ease. Keep the book open on that page until each, and every one of those little playing principles becomes one of those helpful habits that collectively will benefit your playing, and secure an excellent technical foundation through which you can express your musicianship.

Become a Musical Athlete!

The difference between doing a small amount of daily practice, as opposed to cramming your work into one long session the night before your lesson, is far greater than you may think!

Please consider that you are dealing with the muscles around the mouth when practising. In the beginning, your mouth will feel strange as the muscles have not been used in this way before but they will become firm and toned over time. The clarinet player needs strong but sensitive mouth muscles to manipulate the reed and enhance the sound.

Think about how athletes train for major events. They don't do just one or two marathon training sessions a week and nothing on the other days – their muscles would only give way! They work evenly throughout the week to consistently build their muscles and increase their stamina over time.

Can you imagine practising a one-off marathon on your clarinet? Your lower lip would be sore and bitten in no time, and your sound would be tight! I am certain that one of the best ways to getting yourself to long-term success is to **keep yourself motivated by witnessing small amounts of progress daily**. Taking baby steps at first – and lots of them – will bring you the results you want, and you will have great fun and enjoy a sense of satisfaction and achievement along the way.

From now on consider yourself a 'musical athlete'. You will **practise for a small amount of time on a regular basis**. Your mouth will then develop sensitivity to support the reed and you will develop your 'lip'!

The 'Lip'

The term 'lip' is referred to by clarinet players all the time as they constantly talk about it and are aware of its condition. They are of course speaking about the bottom lip. Their 'lip' is a piece of their equipment for playing, and they take care of it just as a dentist would look after one of his tools.

An excellent tip to build up your lip strength is to keep the clarinet assembled out of its case. You can then pick it up at random times during the day when you have spare moments and play six or seven strong long notes. You will become accustomed to the feeling of the clarinet in your mouth and will sense the strength building up in your lip as it becomes easier and easier to produce an open, round sound.

I would especially recommend keeping the clarinet out to young beginners. The long note exercise takes the same amount of time it takes for a beginner to assemble the instrument. Providing the clarinet is looked after in a safe place, away from young siblings and stray dogs it will come to no harm at all. Remember to dry it out after playing.

Don't Want to Play?

Some days you may simply not want to play! Fair enough, have a day off and start again tomorrow! You will have done no harm. Watch out, though! If you catch yourself wanting to take too many 'days off', have some compassion for your 'lip', which will suffer later because of its neglect. Remember the musical stars that you aspire to play like – imagine sounding just like them!

What Exactly to Practise?

Playing versus practising

We all love to play the tunes that we have already learned because it feels amazing to do so. We enjoy the sound that comes out of the instrument, and the compliments that we receive from family members who are enjoying our playing. They add to our confidence and satisfaction making the experience extra special. When it comes to actual practising, **working on those things you can't play well, will reap so much better rewards than spending your time on tunes that you can**. Playing what you can, is playing to maintain a standard – whereas **practising to improve, puts a whole new complexion on things**.

Take time to enjoy playing your favourite accomplishments at the end of your exercise session, but **spend most of your time learning new exercises and tunes, stretching yourself and improving your ability** all round.

Not much time to practise – are you certain?

Even on those days when there's little time for practice, ask yourself if there are five minutes you could spare. If you're honest, the chances are that you will find five minutes. **It is so much better to play a little something, rather than nothing to keep your embouchure muscles toned and keep the sound production easy.** During busy days find five minutes to practise your long notes, because they reap the most benefits in the shortest amount of time.

A practice routine

Having a plan of how you spend your practice time and exactly what you're going to practise will reap good rewards and get you moving faster. Your objectives are to develop your musicianship and technical expertise together. The 'Daily Practice Plan for All Round Development' embraces a comprehensive array of skills and will steer you to:

- Play with a pulse so you bring your music to life.
- Develop your technique.
- Improve the sound.
- Develop your listening skills.
- Read music with confidence.
- Be observant and feel appreciative of your successes.

Don't be tempted to take short cuts and omit parts of the plan. Follow it in sequence to reap the benefits.

As the title indicates it's ideal that you follow it daily. Being realistic, this may not be possible during a busy week. Simply play long notes for five minutes on the days you can't manage a full session. Providing you keep going and do not stop during those 5 minutes, you will keep your embouchure in good condition. Remember to ask yourself your Sensible Sound Questions to get the most benefit from those precious minutes.

FOCUS
CONCENTRATE
LISTEN

'Daily Practice Plan for All Round Development'

1. The 'hands-on clarinet exercise' – 2 minutes.

Before you even play one note, spend well invested time to 'feel' your fingers on the whole body of the clarinet. Focus especially on the right-hand fingers. Exercise them on the lower holes and keys. This hand tends to get neglected at the beginning. It gets stuck in contorted positions and then it has problems getting in the best place when the fingers are needed in the future. For revision see 'Let's Get Hands-On', Chapter 2.

2. 'The long note exercise' – 5 minutes – essential!

Play a selection of long notes for five minutes. **Do not stop** to give yourself a rest in the middle. **Keep going to tone the embouchure.**

Ask your **Sensible Sound Questions** and LISTEN:

- Is my sound sweet and pure?
- Is my sound wobbly or even?
- Is my sound keeping at the same pitch or is it going up and getting sharp – or is it going down and getting flat?

With careful listening, you'll be surprised what you can hear, and as a result, how you start to control the air column to improve the sound quality. Read 'The Best Tone Exercises' in Chapter 3 for extra revision.

3. Flexibility and technical exercises – play for as long as you can.

Your personal tutor book will be full of these. Go to the page in your tutor book that introduces the new notes you are studying and you will find lots of exercises that you can play.

4. Scales and arpeggios – more than 5 minutes.

As soon as you are technically able to play scale and arpeggio patterns, slot them into your daily practice routine. Play them rhythmically and evenly with the pulse and feel the notes of the scale flowing and sitting in the groove of the beat.

5. Learn new pieces – spend as much time as you can.

Remember to breathe with the phrases, play with a pulse and observe all the musical signs and symbols written on the part.

Practical How to Practise Tips

Want to keep smiling? Get the best out of your practice time – no messing about! **Intelligent practice gets quick and positive results.**

- **Practise the 'Sound Production Procedure':**

1. **Set the embouchure** – rest the reed on the lower overturned lip and put the top teeth on the mouthpiece.
2. Relax the lips to **take the air in through the sides of the mouth.**
3. **Tongue the tip of the reed** to start the note as you **push a continuous stream of air through the clarinet.**

- **Follow the**

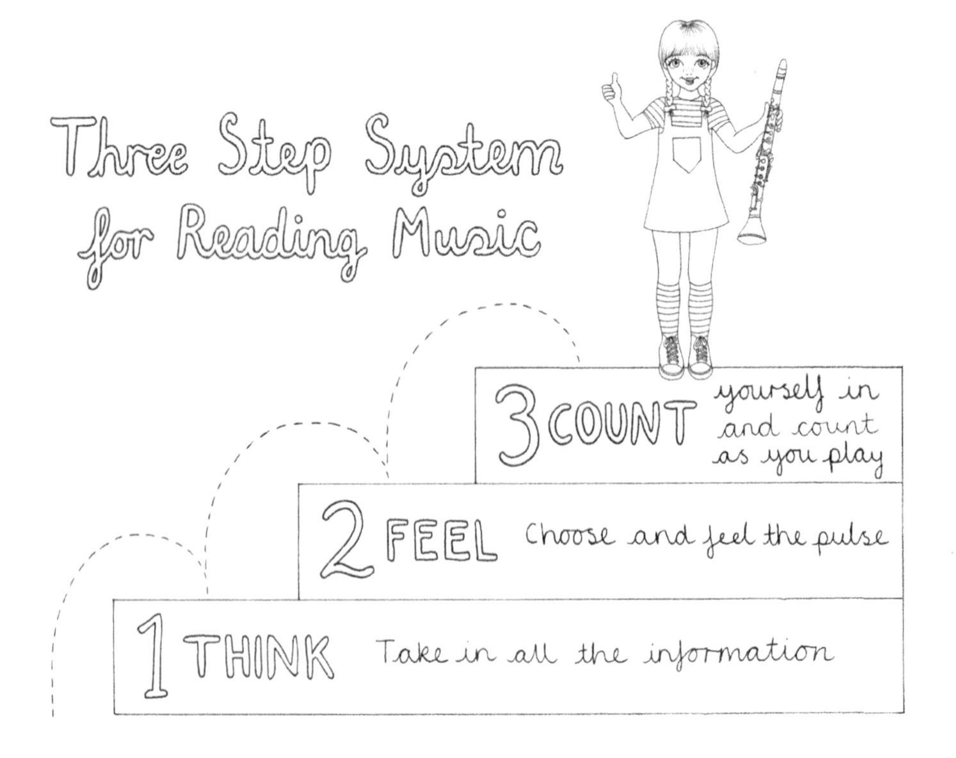

- **Allow the embouchure to strengthen naturally** – do not force the sound even if it means practising within a certain range of notes for a while.

- **Practise away from distractions** – e.g. incoming texts, annoying brothers or sisters, the television, the cat!

- **Focus!** A small amount of focused, structured exercising is better than playing randomly for longer. Give each note your full 100% attention - do not think about what's for dinner!

- **Make your best sound every time!**

- **Listen!** You will know when the playing is sounding good and where you need to go back and practise a passage again. You will also know when the music feels right, when it is flowing and full of life - because **you always play with a pulse and you always play with energy and enthusiasm!**

The 'Practising Checklist for Beginners'
Keep this open near your music stand!

Instrument assembly – make sure:

- The bridge keys on the middle joints are perfectly joined.
- The reed is straight and set to the tip of the mouthpiece.
- The mouthpiece and reed are lined up with the long speaker key at the back of the clarinet.
- The reed is moist (not soggy).
- The ligature does not nip the reed. It is placed central to the mouthpiece with its top edge underneath the straight line from which the reed has been shaved.

Your posture when standing – make sure:

- Your feet are slightly apart and rooted sturdily to the ground.
- Your back is straight.

Your posture when sitting – make sure:

- Your feet are rooted to the floor and slightly apart.
- Your back is straight, sitting up from the base of the spine and forms a right angle with the top of the legs.

The sling – make sure:

- The neckpiece is as low on the neck as possible and over the clothing.
- The sling is at the best length and your neck is not straining to reach the mouthpiece.

Holding the clarinet – make sure:

- The clarinet is held about 40° from the body. The shoulders, arms and wrist are relaxed. The elbows are low, and the arms are slightly forward not touching the sides of the body.
- The mouthpiece is coming to you – you are not stretching your neck to get it in your mouth.
- The right-hand thumb is straight underneath the thumb rest and touches the thumb rest between the nail and the knuckle.

- Both hands are in a 'C' position around the clarinet keeping away from the side keys near the first fingers.
- The middle fingers are almost at right angles to the instrument.
- All the fingers arch and are held near the keys.
- The fingers pads press the holes and ring keys firmly.

Your mouth – make sure:

- The reed rests firmly on the pink of the lip, at the junction where the mouthpiece leaves the reed.
- You haven't put too much face into your mouth, and your bottom lip has disappeared.
- Your chin is 'flat,' not bunching upwards towards the reed. Think 'jaw to floor'.
- You are making a slight 'smile' at the mouth corners.
- The clarinet is not wobbling in the mouth. The top teeth anchor to the top of the mouthpiece.
- You are not puffing the cheeks.

Making the sound – make sure:

- You relax the sides of the mouth to breathe in.
- You allow the air to flow through the mouthpiece and do not bite.
- You tongue the reed and push an EVEN column of air through the instrument.
- You tongue repeatedly to make a series of notes.
- You do not use individual puffs of air to make the notes.
- You do not breathe in through your nose or suck up the air through the clarinet.
- Your sound is even and sweet and does not wobble or vary in pitch.

The music – make sure:

- You can see the music without moving the head up or down (and moving the angle of the clarinet in the mouth).
- The stand is just under head height.
- The music is far enough away from you so you can hold the clarinet out correctly.

Amazing Attitude! Bring it on!

Decide to be confident and positive for the best results

- **Let your playing evolve**. Technical strength and musicianship mature with experience.
- **Notice and admire the improvements** in each practice session.
- **Keep upbeat**. If things are not working out, remember that they can be fixed.
- **Waste no time on frustration!** Do not put the clarinet in the bin, throw it against a wall, or burn it. Take a deep breath and **find the solution**. Consult the 'Practising Checklist for Beginners' in this chapter, and the chapter 'Whoops! Got a Problem?'.
- **Be happy – enjoy every minute**. Love every single tune you play!

When little practising happens, the absolute worst happens – you grow to hate playing because every single time you take the instrument out of its case, it's difficult to play!

With lots of practice, the most wonderful thing happens – you grow to love playing the clarinet! It will be responsive and easy to play, and you will produce that hot sound that you admire so much!

PRACTICE REALLY IS MAGIC!

Happy practising – have fun!

On a Final Note

Access your FREE online video course 'Clarinet Kickstart' here!

'Clarinet Kickstart' is the perfect accompaniment to this book, as it will supplement your learning from a visual perspective.

At 1 hour 20 minutes long, this series of fun, animated videos are niched into one easy to follow package. It will give you the vital facts about the beginning stages of learning. Step by step, this audio-visual material will make your playing easy and enjoyable – it is like having a teacher in your living room helping you along the way!

The course echoes parts of the book, focusing on specific areas in turn: the clarinet itself, how it is handled, how the sound is made, how to read music with understanding, and how to feel and play with a pulse.

At the end, all these skills are brought together when you get the chance to play beginner tunes along with fabulous accompaniments.

Wishing You Every Success

I hope you have enjoyed every stage of this book. It has been my absolute pleasure to be a part of your learning.

If you have followed all the little exercises through, along the way, you have launched the beginning of your exciting musical journey with the core, basic tools you need to develop your playing.

You know how to:

- Assemble the clarinet and reed correctly
- Handle the instrument securely
- Adopt the best posture for breathing
- Control your embouchure
- Articulate the reed
- Control the air you push through the clarinet
- Feel the pulse
- Count and play rhythmically
- Breathe with the phrasing

These are, of course, your fundamental skills which are vital during every stage of your learning in the future. Put the book aside for now in the confidence that you can go back and revise them at any time.

Remember that your skills are only a vehicle for making music. You are now a creative artist so put your whole attention on how the music **feels** and communicate with your listener. Focus on the natural flow of the breath, and play with the natural phrasing and pulse of the music. Your playing will flow and feel wholesome.

Keep going when you experience a challenge. Never give up, and *never let anyone tell you that you are not musical!*

Most of all – **aspire high and enjoy every single note of music on your journey!**

Goodbye for now!

Check out our website: http://takenote-music.co.uk

Printed in Great Britain
by Amazon